WORD

Also by John Silverlight
THE VICTORS' DILEMMA: ALLIED INTERVENTION IN THE
RUSSIAN CIVIL WAR

WORDS

JOHN SILVERLIGHT

in association with
THE OBSERVER

First published 1985 by
THE MACMILLAN PRESS LTD
London and Basingstoke
Companies and representatives
throughout the world

Set in Palatino by Columns of Reading

Printed in Hong Kong

British Library Cataloguing in Publication Data

Silverlight, John
  Words.
  1. English language – Usage
  I. Title   II. The Observer
  428.1   PE1460

  ISBN 0–333–38010–X
  ISBN 0–333–38011–8 Pbk

INTRODUCTION

The seeds of this collection of articles were sown one day in the late 1960s by an articulated lorry roaring past my house. At first I merely felt irritation, then I wondered, why 'articulated'? 'Articulate', I thought, meant able to express oneself, but what did that have to do with this noisy great brute? The Shorter Oxford provided the answer. The verb 'articulate' did indeed mean to express oneself, but a much earlier sense was to attach by a joint: an articulated lorry was one with a joint. 'Articulate' was derived from an old root *ar-* : to join; so was the Latin *ars* : art or craft.

Some months earlier I had begun work on a book on the Allied intervention in the Russian civil war, a confused and confusing episode. It was not easy just to sort out in my own mind the main events and their consequences, let alone organise the material into a coherent, readable narrative − unlike most of the hundreds of books I was having to read, plus the mountains of official documents. The experience did not do much for life at home or at *The Observer*, but it taught me something about writing. As I worked on, more and more despairingly, it seemed that what I was trying to do was like nothing so much as a job of carpentry, or rather joinery: fitting bits together so that the joins were not noticeable or, if they did show, they were not too obvious.

So there I was, slogging away at 1919, not making much progress, when this lorry came thundering by, sending me to the dictionary − and to the discovery that my vaguely formulated thoughts about joining were absolutely right. That is what writing is about. The comparison still comforts me today, even if I don't find the job any easier, whether it is a 200 000-word book, a 2000-word article, or the 200-word or 300-word pieces collected here.

The opportunity to express the interest in words aroused that day came in 1979 when the Editor of *The Observer*, Donald Trelford, suggested that as part of a series of background articles I was doing on current events I might occasionally write about words − new, difficult, misused, whatever; one he had in mind was 'parameter'. It took nearly two years, by which time 'Words' had become a regular feature in the paper, to work up the nerve to take it on.

One of the first pieces was on the confusion, thanks to their similar appearance, of 'deprecate' (from *de*, down or against, and *precari* to pray), to disapprove of, and 'depreciate' (from *de* and *pretium*, price), to belittle. Rather pleased with the little polemic I had knocked out, I showed the draft, over lunch at Antoine's in Charlotte Street, to Professor Randolph Quirk, then Quain Professor of English Literature and Language at University College, London, now Vice-Chancellor of London University.

'Very good, very good', he said. 'But if you'll forgive my saying so, you sound a bit like an Eastbourne colonel.' The two words, he said, share an area of 'semantic overlap', and then, very patiently, he explained how it had evolved. At first 'deprecate' meant ward off by prayer (the meaning of the Latin *deprecari*) and 'depreciate', decline in value; later the first took on the sense of protest against, and the second, cause decline in value; so to the not-so-different senses, to express disapproval of ('deprecate') and to disparage ('depreciate'). The piece, when it appeared in print, was a good deal less emphatic than the draft.

But although that lesson was as crucial as the discovery about 'articulate' and 'art', I still yearned, if less hotly, to say, 'This is correct; this, in contrast, is incorrect.' I owe my final cure of the itch for certainty to Dr Robert Burchfield, Chief Editor of the Oxford English Dictionaries. 'English grammar', he writes in *The Spoken Word: a BBC Guide*, 'is a complicated system never quite mastered by the best speakers of English. The best writers and speakers avoid grammatical solecisms by keeping clear of areas which contain problems that would reveal their own uncertainties.'

Even before that booklet was published, Dr Burchfield had explained to me how he saw his job of editing the Supplements to the Oxford English Dictionary. Like the great Sir James Murray and his fellow OED editors, he was recording the history of the English language; he was not telling people how to use that language. My own approach now became clear to me. I was never going to be (in Dr Conor Cruise O'Brien's phrase) a lord of lexicography, such as Professor Quirk or Dr Burchfield. What I could do was report on usage and its changes.

I am also much indebted to Professor A. C. Gimson, Emeritus Professor of Phonetics at University College, London. Faced with the opposite of unanimity among dictionaries about the pronunciation of 'controversy' (con*trov*ersy or *cont*roversy?), I consulted a lexicographer friend. 'Let's see what "Gimson" says', she replied. ' "Gimson"?' 'Everyman's English Pronouncing Dictionary – A. C. Gimson's the editor.' That was my introduction to a book that has been invaluable – and to a person whose help has been equally so. Certainty, as I now know, is unattainable. Authority is rare, but if one looks hard enough it can be found. Professor Gimson has it. (As for 'controversy', both pronunciations are equally common.)

There are still more debts: to Mrs Lesley Burnett, who after working with Dr Burchfield on the OED Supplements is revising the Shorter Oxford; to Miss Valerie Adams, Lecturer in English at University College, London, and colleague of Professor Quirk in the English Language Survey there; to *Observer* colleagues, especially Trevor Grove; to my wife and two sons; most of all perhaps to readers of *The Observer*, who, almost from the start of the column, have been responding to it, favourably, unfavourably, always helpfully.

A word on presentation. The entries are in alphabetical order because it seemed a more helpful way of arranging them than in, say, subjects (I suspect many of them would defy categorization) or the order in which they appeared. However, they remain journalism. They were undertaken seriously in the hope that they would inform and entertain, not in order to instruct: this book is in no sense a would-be dictionary or 'guide'. It is a collection of articles, some fairly timeless but many of them reflecting what was happening when they were written – the Falklands fighting, for instance. So, rather than try to edit out such expressions as 'last week', 'last month', 'recently', etc., the entries have been dated. It can be taken that undated material was added by the author while the collection was being prepared for book form.

ACID RAIN. The Rev. C. F. Warren, of Machen, near Newport, says he has heard that this expression was first used in 1872. Geoffrey Lean, *The Observer*'s Science Correspondent, agrees: the chemist Robert Angus Smith coined it in his book *Air and Rain* published in that year, claiming that the acid air in Manchester bleached fabrics and acid rain damaged vegetation.

Scientists say 'acid rain' is an oversimplification: acid is carried in rain, gases and in clouds and fog. But the term is powerfully evocative and there is no easy alternative. A possibility, says Mr Lean, is 'acid fallout'.

16 OCTOBER 1983

ACUMEN. Browsing in a book on words by the American columnist William Safire, *On Language* (published in the US), I was surprised to read that while most people prefer the pronunciation *a*cumen, ac*u*men 'is preferred by lexicographers'. Surely not, I thought, and went to my dictionaries. Collins and Longman showed *a*cumen first, as I expected. However, the Concise Oxford and the American Webster's showed only ac*u*men. Worse still, Everyman's English Pronouncing Dictionary showed ac*u*men as the preferred pronunciation.

Someone I think of as embodying the people on whom Daniel Jones based the first (1917) edition of the Everyman dictionary — Southern English families 'whose menfolk were educated at the great public boarding schools' — said, 'I would never dream of saying it that way.' Another woman, less well educated but with an instinct for pronunciation, said, 'I wouldn't know what you meant if you said ac*u*men.' Recently (see PRONUNCIATION) I wrote that in an uncertain world 'Gimson' — Professor A. C. Gimson is the dictionary's present editor — 'is a great comfort.' He is, but I am worried about this one. So, I gather, is he, even to the extent of considering revising the entry in the next edition.

6 SEPTEMBER 1981

1

AMELIORATION.

Some twenty years ago I was proud to describe myself as permissive. Now, thanks to the word's 'worsening' in meaning (see PEJORATION), as in 'permissive society', I would hesitate to do so. Brooding on these matters, I had the feeling that pejoration was more common than the opposite process, amelioration. An English don persuaded me that this was indeed only a feeling. Here are three examples of amelioration. 'Fond', in its first OED definition, is 'insipid': 'If the salt be fonnyd it is not worthy' — Wycliffe, 1388. 'Nice' is 'foolish, stupid, senseless'. 'Shrewd' is 'depraved, wicked, malignant'.

Jean Aitchison, of the London School of Economics, writes in her paperback *Language Change: Progress or Decay* (Fontana) that 'there is no evidence that language is either progressing or decaying. Disruption and therapy seem to balance one another in a perpetual stalemate.' Quite. As I have come to feel more and more strongly: change, yes; decay, no.

(Caxton, Jean Aitchison writes, held the moon responsible for change. 'And certaynly our langage now vsed varyeth ferre from that which was vsed and spoken whan I was borne. For we englysshe men ben borne vnder the domynacyon of the mone, which is neuer stedfaste but euer wauerynge one season and dycreaseth another season.')

5 JUNE 1982

ANIMALS

(and judges). Why do so many magistrates and judges describe violence as animal-like behaviour? When some youths appeared in a Brighton court after August Bank Holiday disturbances, the chairman said to one of them: 'You behave like animals, you must expect to be herded like animals.' Whatever the youth did, if he was guilty of unprovoked violence, he was not acting like most animals: practically the only species that attacks its own kind without provocation is Man.

Even more offensive is the judge who tells a man convicted of rape that he has behaved like an animal. Again, males of practically every species except ours approach females only when they have unmistakably signalled that they are ready for mating.

20 SEPTEMBER 1981

ANIMALS (unusual).

Sandbach's Dictionary of Astonishing British Animals is the latest title in a series of 'micro-tomelets' (the word was coined by the *Times Literary Supplement* some years ago) published by J. L. Carr. Entries include:

'**Dick Whittington's Cat** is portrayed on the cover of this book [in a print of Whittington], indisputable proof that his tale is true.'

'**Charles Kingsley's Wasp**, saved by the author from drowning, afterwards lived in a cleft in his dressing room wall.'

'**Ronald**, having led and, astonishingly, survived the Charge of the Light Brigade . . . was put to pasture quite close to this publisher's office [in Kettering]. His head and tail may be seen . . . during the summer months.'

'**Wessex**, d. 1927, a rough-haired terrier, having bitten several eminent literary critics, was rewarded by Florence Hardy with an expensive wireless set.'

The author, Mr R. G. E. Sandbach, is a retired museum curator.

There are errors. A dog (Lyon) is mentioned as having been 'present at Lord Byron's death at the Battle of Missolonghi (1824)'. Byron died of a fever that year in besieged Missolonghi during the Greek War of Independence; the battle — when the Greeks tried unsuccessfully to break out — took place in 1825. And in the entry on Barnum's elephant Jumbo I was sorry not to see the jingle, 'Jumbo said to Alice, "I love you";/Alice said to Jumbo, "I don't believe you do./If you really loved me, as you say you do,/You wouldn't go to Yankeeland/And leave me in the Zoo." '

But these are minor faults. The book is a tiny treasure, just right for, say, the birthday of one of those awkward friends who have everything.

21 AUGUST 1983

APPEASEMENT.

'We have also had to struggle against the appeasers of the Foreign Office' — *Daily Mail*, 5 June. 'This insidious minefield of compromise and appeasement' — *Daily Mail*, 15 June. No doubt about it: 'appeasement' is a thoroughly dirty word, has been ever since Neville Chamberlain returned from Munich on 30 September 1938. It was not always so. In

3

1929 J. M. Keynes wrote approvingly of Winston Churchill as an 'ardent . . .advocate of . . . appeasement . . . in Germany, in Ireland, in Turkey'. Just a decade later the *New Statesman* was writing of 'proposals that smell of appeasement' (both examples from Volume I of A Supplement to the Oxford English Dictionary).

Writing about PEJORATION and AMELIORATION (see entries) I had the impression that both processes were arbitrary. A closer look at examples in the OED has made me think again: 'The iuste goddis neuer appease theyr yres [ires, angers] against vniuste men' (1534). Here I detect a note of disparagement. That note is even stronger in Johnson's 'to appease enmity by blandishment and bribes' (1750). I now think that words that undergo pejoration or amelioration have within them from the start the potential for such change. Predestination?

4 JULY 1982

ARGENTINE/-IAN. In line three of its admirable 'Portrait of the Week' the current *Spectator* refers to 'Argentinian forces', in line seven to 'the Argentine navy', in line 22 to the 'Argentinian fleet', and in line 34 to 'Argentinian insistence'. Overpage Ferdinand Mount refers eleven times to 'Argentinian' or 'Argentinians', once to 'Anglo-Argentine negotiations' and once to 'Anglo-Argentinian projects'. Final score in the whole issue: '-ian' 15, '-ine' 9, 'Argie' 1.

The *Spectator* is one of our more literate journals, but as a weekly it has time to polish its prose. Dailies and evenings, with four or five hours between going to press and starting work, can be forgiven for the occasional slip. Loyal to *The Observer* though I am, I would not bet on its consistency.

There is no doubt as to which is 'correct'. The country calls itself *Republica Argentina* – in English, Argentine Republic, less formally the Argentine or Argentina. Logically-minded folk insist that since the word 'Argentine' is an adjective, to call its people 'Argentinians' is like saying 'Germanians'. But usage notoriously defies logic, and the useful Oxford Dictionary for Writer and Editors says that 'Argentinian' is tending to replace 'Argentine'. Dining with friends two nights ago I went round the table asking which they used. Six said '-ian'; one (whose mother tongue is Hungarian) said '-ine'. The dictionary could be right.

25 APRIL 1982

ASHES. A hundred years ago today Australia for the first time beat England (by seven runs) in a test match on English soil. On 2 September the *Sporting Times* carried a notice, 'In affectionate remembrance of English Cricket which died at The Oval, 29th August 1882 . . . The body will be cremated and the Ashes taken to Australia.'

All that is generally known. Less so perhaps, at least to non-cricket fans, is the fact that real ashes do exist. They came into being, says Wisden, in 1883 when England won the series and 'some Melbourne women burnt a bail used in the third game' and presented the ashes, in an urn, to the England captain. They are now kept permanently at Lord's. (That explains why the Concise Oxford has changed its definition of 'the Ashes'. The sixth edition (1976) had 'imaginary trophy for winner of series of test matches between England and Australia'. In the seventh edition, which came out last month, 'imaginary' has been deleted.)

For years people have been arguing about what was in the urn — the remains of a bail? a stump? a bat? Even a jock-strap has been suggested (were jock-straps worn in the early 1880s?). An article in the August issue of *The Cricketer* said it was a ball. And on Friday, in the latest issue of the magazine, a letter said the urn was accidentally knocked over some years before it went to Lord's; the contents were replaced by ordinary wood-ash.

29 AUGUST 1982

AS/LIKE. When I was young, say in my early teens, I was not too clear about such things as conjunctions (e.g. 'as') and prepositions (e.g. 'like'), but I was highly, intolerantly, aware of the difference between those two words. One said (if one were impolite enough), 'He eats like a pig', or, 'He eats as a pig eats.' One did not say, 'He eats like a pig eats.'

To some people interchanging the two words is still

anathema. I am not so sure, though it does jar on me. Four dictionaries accept 'like' as a conjunction, two with slight reservations: the Concise Oxford describes it as 'colloq.' and the Longmans Dictionary of Contemporary English as 'infml'; Collins has no reservation; nor has the American Webster's New Collegiate, which quotes Keats: 'They raven down scenery like children do sweetmeats.'

That doughtiest of rearguard fighters, Kingsley Amis, commenting on the Concise Oxford example, 'cannot do it like you do', agreed that he would probably not *say* 'as you do'. But saying it, he insisted, was not writing it.

1 FEBRUARY 1981

AUTHOR. Sir James Goldsmith's offer of £50 000 for 'the best

investigative journalism into subversion in the media' has predictably aroused controversy. I am concerned not with the merits or otherwise of the offer but with the wording of the announcement. In his letter to *The Times* on 16 September Sir James wrote: 'The journalist Peter Shipley . . . authored a document in which he described extremist and revolutionary groups in Britain and the funding of their publications.'

Leave aside the use of 'author' as a verb (it does appear as such in dictionaries although it is particularly unhappy here). What worries me is 'document': 'a piece of paper, booklet etc., providing information, esp. of an official or legal nature' (Collins). Webster's definition of the verb 'to document' includes, 'To equip statements with exact references to authoritative supporting information.'

A journalist documents an article by citing the documents on which his arguments or assertions are based — Mr Shipley does so with a 'List of References' on the back page of his pamphlet. The journalist does not himself write (or author) the documents.

27 SEPTEMBER 1981

AUTHORESS. In 1815 Jane Austen wrote to the Domestic

Chaplain to the Prince of Wales, 'I think I may boast myself . . . the most unlearned and uninformed female who ever dared to be an authoress.' In 1885, however, in its article on the word, the OED noted that it was used 'only when sex is purposely emphasised'. Otherwise, and especially in the sense of 'female literary composer', 'author' was used of both sexes. Indeed, the suffix '-ess' was already then going out generally for words denoting profession or occupation.

Some '-ess' words survive, including, surprisingly, 'authoress': twice in the *Spectator* and once in *The Observer* in the past few months. But there are fewer and fewer of them; among those that have disappeared are 'doctress' and 'editress'. One that is usually cited as being 'necessary' is 'actress'. Many women in the theatre prefer 'actor', and Anthony Powell, in *The Strangers All Are Gone*, the fourth volume of his memoirs, describes the word as 'slightly suspect'. I asked him why. It goes back to his youth. His parents would use the word 'actressy' of someone they disapproved of; a tart in the dock would often say she was 'an actress'.

Mr Powell would not condemn '-ess' words in general and he quoted 'Queen and huntress, chaste and fair.' Of course; one would not rewrite Ben Jonson. But that apart, when are such words necessary? Dame Elizabeth Frink, asked about the word 'sculptress', said roundly that it was used 'only by the ignorant'. I once used the expression 'life peeress' when talking to Lady Wootton about an article she was writing for *The Observer*. Women in the Upper House, she said gently but firmly, are life peers.

6 FEBRUARY 1984

M. Grant Cormack, of Belfast, dislikes 'poetess' even more that 'authoress'. She writes that a woman poet she knew 'used to quote wryly: "The poet and the poetess/The little more − the little less." ' Of seven desk dictionaries I have just looked at, only one, the Longman Dictionary of Contemporary English (which is primarily aimed at foreign students) notes that 'poetess' is 'now rare'.

13 FEBRUARY 1983

AZANIA is the imaginary African country of Evelyn Waugh's *Black Mischief*. I have just learnt that it is also the name for

South Africa used by the Black Consciousness Movement (brainchild of the late Steve Biko) and its white sympathisers such as Nadine Gordimer.

29 MAY 1983

Ramsgate, Kent

DEAR SIR, *The Name 'Azania' was not invented by Evelyn Waugh. He must have taken it from the name by which Greco-Roman geographers and merchants knew the area of East Africa open to western trade: roughly the modern Tanzania. See, for example, J. Innes Miller, The Spice Trade of the Roman Empire, pp. 163–8.*

Yours sincerely

J. D. RENWICK

BALL.

A potent word and one with an astonishing range of meanings, especially slang. Entries in Eric Partridge's Dictionary of Slang include: 'having a ball' for having a really good time; 'on the ball' as a description of someone who is alert and efficient; 'ball of fire' which, in the nineteenth century, meant a glass of brandy but now means 'a notably energetic and effectual person (usually male), often sarcastically in negative'.

There are less delicate uses: 'to balls something up', US 'to ball up' (more recently 'to ball' in the US also has the sense 'to have sexual intercourse', 'usually considered vulgar', says Webster's Collegiate); 'balls to you' (which a French dictionary of English slang published in the 1920s translates as 'zut pour vous'). 'Balls' in this sense, like the diminutive 'bollocks', is described in dictionaries as 'taboo slang' or 'vulg'. But for centuries 'ballocks' (the original spelling) was standard English for testicles. The Oxford English Dictionary quotes John Wycliffe, 'All beeste that . . . kitte [cut] and taken awey the ballokes is' (1382). It was still respectable when Queen Victoria was on the throne. (In the eighteenth century, according to Grose's Dictionary of the Vulgar Tongue, first published in 1785, 'ballocks' also meant a parson. Partridge, quoting Arthur Bryant's book on Pepys, *Saviour of the Navy*, says this sense 'may be at least a century older, for in 1684 the Officer

Commanding the Straits Fleet always referred to his chaplain as Ballocks'.)

Less delicate still is the ribald Second World War song, to the tune of 'Colonel Bogey':

Hitler has only got one ball,
Goering has two but very small,
Himmler's got something sim'lar,
And poor old Goebbels
[pronunciation adjusted for emphasis and rhyme]
has no balls at all.

However, when describing the word as potent I was not thinking of mere ribaldry. Rather I had in mind Andrew Marvell's 'To His Coy Mistress', with its gorgeous implicit but vibrant sexuality:

Let us roll all our Strength and all
Our sweetness up into one Ball.

It is nice to think that one result of our having a ball could be that widows and orphans of former colleagues have more of a ball than they might otherwise have had.

Written for the 1982 Press Ball organised by the City of London branch of the National Union of Journalists.

BIEN PENSANT. Is this the new fashionable term of abuse? It appeared on successive days last month in *The Times* and *The Listener*. In the first, Bernard Levin wrote about 'one of the most influential *bien-pensants* behind the Labour Party's educational policies', who said during a television discussion that 'he didn't know what the word "excellent" meant'. In *The Listener*, the historian John Roberts, reviewing Hugh Thomas's *An Unfinished History of the World*, wrote '*Bien-pensant* progressives would not approve. A story which culminates in a recognition of the primacy of place that any liberal must accord the United States, warts and all, risks rejection before it is read.'

The expression is not easy to translate. It began as an ironic description of an important part of the French bourgeoisie, especially in the provinces, as seen by French intellectuals: rigidly Roman Catholic in religion and right-wing in politics, orthodox conformist, stuffy – *La Grande Peur des Bien-pensants*, a fierce attack by the Catholic anti-fascist writer Georges Bernanos on French middle-class materialism, appeared in 1931. The interesting twist by Mr Levin and Mr Roberts is to turn it against people who, unlike the original targets, are left-wing and, by implication, intellectuals.

Harmless enough, I suppose. But I wondered how many of their readers understood the expression. I asked five colleagues what it meant. Four, all graduates, did not know. The fifth, who left school at 14, did.

See PUTTING ON DOG.

23 DECEMBER 1979

Bottom LINE.

On 12 May, under the headline 'The Bottom Line of Diplomacy', the *Guardian* said in a leading article: 'If we are to make open war with Argentina with Parliament's assent, then we must know the bottom lines of diplomacy. What, in short, are we going to war about.' The meaning was clear enough, but the expression was new to me. It looked like accountant's language, so I consulted our Company Secretary. He knows the expression although he does not use it himself. It is American and is literally the bottom line of a company's annual financial statement: the amount of profit, after tax, available for distribution among the shareholders.

This was confirmed by an American dictionary, Webster's New Twentieth Century Unabridged (confusingly, it has nothing to do with *the* Webster's Third New International), which said the expression also meant 'the basic or most important factor . . . (slang)'. An American colleague says she remembers hearing it 15 years ago on the *Wall Street Journal*, admittedly a financial newspaper, 'but the use was in the sense of "nitty gritty" '.

Now I am meeting it all the time. On Tuesday Peter Hobday used in the *Guardian* sense on BBC TV's 'Newsnight'. The Tuesday before, in a Radio 3 feature on one-parent families, an American professor of sociology said, 'That's the bottom line, isn't it', when speaking of 'how the children are getting on' in such families. I am told that Treasury officials use it to describe the minimum terms they would settle for when engaged in negotiations, domestic or international.

27 JUNE 1982

C ARDINAL.

Some years ago, writing about the Russian Civil War, I was feverishly trying to find the word to describe the difference between *recognition* by the Great Powers of a White Russian regime and *support* for it. 'All important'? 'Crucial'? 'Vital'? None of them seemed right. I think I settled for 'vital' and pressed on, but it kept nagging me, distracting me. Then, days later, up from the subconscious swam 'cardinal'. It looked and felt right, but what was a Prince of the Roman Catholic Church doing in that *galère*? Derivation provided the answer: 'cardinal' comes from the Latin *cardo*, *cardinis*, that upon which something hinges.

Last September the historian Noble Frankland wrote in *The Times* apropos the Battle of Britain, 'There was another cardinal, indeed sovereign, factor, radar.' I would have transposed the two words if I had used them both: for me in this context a cardinal outranks a sovereign. But there is no argument about the word's expressing supreme importance. I ration myself to using it once a year, if as often.

24 MAY 1981

C ATCH 22.

Two readers, Rita Keenan, of Shepherds Bush, in west London, and A. Thompson, of Salford, ask about Catch 22. Perhaps it is worth quoting in context. It is the title of Joseph Heller's great comic novel. The hero is Captain Yossarian, a US Air Force bombardier (bomb-aimer, not what the Royal Artillery calls a corporal) in the Second World War, whose only ambition is not to fly any more missions. Here he is talking to the group's MO, Doc Daneeka, about getting himself grounded after deciding to go crazy: ' "Can't you ground someone who's crazy?" "Oh, sure, I have to. There's a rule saying I have to ground anyone who's crazy." "Then why can't you ground me? I'm crazy . . ." "Anyone who wants to get out of combat duty isn't really crazy." '

Heller goes on: 'There was only one catch and that was Catch 22. All an aircrew member had to do was ask, and as soon as he did he would no longer be crazy . . . If he flew more missions he was crazy and didn't have to, but if he didn't want to he was sane and had to. Yossarian was moved very deeply by the absolute simplicity of this clause of Catch 22 and let out a respectful whistle. "That's some catch, that Catch 22", he observed. "The best there is", Doc Daneeka agreed.'

One of Webster's definitions of 'catch' is '. . . trickily concealed difficulty designed esp. to take advantage of the unwary (there must be a catch somewhere)'. Catch 22 is certainly that, but much, much more as well with, in Heller's words, its 'spinning reasonableness', the 'elliptical precision about its perfect pairs of parts'. It hurts to see it applied to the common-or-garden kind.

1 MAY 1983

CLADISTICS.

An obscure but interesting word. Among biologists it is explosive: cladists (from the Greek *klados*, a branch; the 'a' is long, as in 'glade') have had the word Marxist flung at them. Cladistics is an element in the current great debate in the scientific world about Darwinism, but the word defies succinct explanation. (The other Darwin war going on, chiefly in the United States, between Creationists and Evolutionists, complicates the scientific debate but is not otherwise involved.) So when, in 1981, a lexicographer at Longman offered me the definition in the forthcoming New Universal Dictionary I gladly accepted. However, a leading cladist at the Natural History Museum, Dr Humphry Greenwood, found it unacceptable. I found *his* definition unintelligible.

I then offered a small prize to readers who produced the most useful definition. A 50-word limit was imposed and, as encouragement, I quoted Dr Johnson: 'Every other author may aspire to praise; the lexicographer can only hope to escape reproach' (Preface to his Dictionary of the English Language). Of the fifteen replies (not a bad response, I am told, considering how specialised a subject it is), nearly all were unintelligible too. An exception was by Dr Christopher Hill, also of the Natural History Museum, who won the £10 book token with: 'A method of biological classification. Groups are defined only by characteristics that distinguish a group from all

12

others and shared by every member of the same group. For instance the group "Seed Plants" encompasses all groups that share the characteristic, "produced by means of seeds".'

The New Universal definition is: 'A theory that describes the relationship between types of organism on the assumption that their sharing of a unique characteristic (e.g. the hair of mammals) possessed by no other organism indicates their descent from a common ancestor.' Quite neat, to the non-expert. But that word 'theory' damns it from the start. Cladistics is a *system* of classification, not a theory. Here is how Dr Greenwood would revise the definition: 'A taxonomic system that groups organisms together on the basis of their all sharing a unique characteristic (e.g. the mammary glands [rather than hair] of mammals) not shared with any other organism.'

As this book goes to press no other dictionary is even in the running. The Collins Concise has: 'A proposed method of grouping animals by measurable likenesses or homologues', which is not only vague but misleading: cladistics is not restricted to animals and it has been around for more than twenty years; the word surfaced – as a pejorative term, incidentally – in the mid-1960s. The American Ninth New Webster's Collegiate has, 'Biological systematics based on phylogenetic relationships', which I also find unhelpful. Chambers and the Concise Oxford do not have it at all – in the files of the Oxford English Dictionaries there is this provisional definition: 'Systematic classification of groups of organisms on the basis of the order of their assumed divergence from ancestral species.' That, says Dr Greenwood, 'takes a lot of thinking about'. He understands it because he knows the background but doesn't think other people will; it is certainly beyond me.

It all seems innocuous enough, so why the fuss? To non-churchmen the difference between transubstantiation and consubstantiation is pretty recondite too, but it is the kind of thing that gave rise to the Wars of Religion. To orthodox taxonomists, cladists are heretics: they make no attempt to demonstrate processes of evolution, but only the patterns (a few, the so-called 'transformed' cladists, even reject evolution as a scientific theory). Heresy arouses strong feelings. People died in the Wars of Religion.

CLASS WAR.

'Defaced by a company of buzzardly (i.e. stupid) peasants' (1576, Alexander Fleming, antiquary and poet); 'Oh what a rogue and peasant slave am I' (1602, Shakespeare); 'You *peasant*' (1981, anonymous wife to husband, using the worst term of abuse in her vocabulary). So much for the image of the peasant. But he has done better than the villein ('a peasant occupier or cultivator entirely subject to a lord' – OED). Webster defines the derived word 'villain' as 'a person of depraved and malevolent character . . . who deliberately plots and does serious harm to others.' In language as in other things the upper classes do seem to have had things their way – look at the OK words associated with them: noble, patrician, generous, aristocratic, gentle.

I like the concept of *noblesse oblige*: 'privilege entails responsibility' in the Concise Oxford's admirably concise translation. The egalitarian in me, however, also likes Collins's comment: 'Often ironic, the supposed obligation of nobility to be honourable and generous.'

(Yeomen have done rather well. People are proud to claim them as forebears; yeomanry regiments are the cavalry of the Territorial Army. Strange. Yeomen were originally servants or attendants in a royal or noble household. I would rather have been a peasant than a yeoman.)

5 JULY 1981

CLERK.

I may have missed it, but in the constant stream of election news being pumped out I have not come across a mention of the man at the heart of it all: the Clerk of the Crown. The great English jurist Blackstone (1723–80) wrote: 'As soon as the parliament is summoned [as it has been, for 15 June, by last weekend's Royal Proclamation], the lord chancellor . . . sends his warrant to the clerk of the crown in chancery [the full title]; who thereupon issues out writs to the sheriff of every county, for the election of all the members to serve for that county . . .' Which, I gather, is more or less what happens nowadays too.

'A mere clerk' is a common put-down. But who could look down on, say, the Clerk of the Crown, or the Clerk of the House of Commons, or his opposite number in the House of

Lords, who (one supposes) has a quieter life but an even grander title, the Clerk of the Parliaments?

Originally the word meant 'clerk in holy orders', then, says the OED, it came to mean 'scholar'. It was Coleridge who introduced the word 'clerisy' into the language: the 'learned men' of a nation, 'whether poets, or philosophers, or scholars'. However, still lurking in the background is that idea of sacred responsibility. This is what gives such terrible force to the title of Julien Benda's pamphlet denouncing French intellectuals of the extreme Right in the 1920s for, so he claimed, subordinating their free intellects to a political cause: *La Trahison des clercs*.

22 MAY 1983

After writing that article I heard the following anecdote. When the House of Commons was rebuilt after being gutted in the Second World War the architect, Sir Giles Scott, was asked to discuss the Clerks' accommodation with them. Scott, not realising just who he was dealing with (the Clerk's task, according to his statutory declaration, is 'to make true entries, remembrances and journals of the things done and passed in the House of Commons'), did not reply.

After some time he was taken to meet the Clerk, Sir Gilbert (later Lord) Campion; with Campion were the Clerk Assistant and Second Clerk Assistant. Clearly these were three very eminent personages. 'I do apologise, gentlemen', Scott exclaimed, 'I thought you were like bank clerks.' What I like about the story is that it illustrates not only the range in status covered by 'clerk' but how images change: people don't talk like that about bank employees nowadays.

Another clerk with a grand title (if not a grand remuneration) is the Rt Rev. John Bickersteth, Bishop of Bath and Wells. As Clerk of the Closet he had to pass on to his fellow bishops last month the Queen's request that scarlet cassocks should be worn only by clergy connected with the Royal Household. Besides presiding over the Royal College of Chaplains, the Clerk's duties include examining works of theology 'whose authors desire to present copies to the Queen'. Salary £6 8s. (formerly 20 gold nobles) a year, paid quarterly.

Also in the OED's list of clerks is the Clerk of the Weather, 'an imaginary functionary humorously supposed to control the state of the weather'. Obviously an old joke, but the latest

Concise Oxford (1982) and Chambers (1983) still carry it.

5 JUNE 1983

COMPUTER TALK.

Operating manuals for *The Observer*'s new telephones speak of 'dial tone', or of 'dialling' a number. The only trouble is, instead of dials there are push-buttons, or keys. So, will 'dial' survive in this context when, eventually, such phones are in general use? ('Dial' already has a competitor. References in the manuals to computerised facilities in the new system instruct the user to 'key' the button involved, thereby 'keying in' the instruction to the computer.)

There is an analogy in printing. Traditionally pages − book, journal, newspaper − are made up on the 'stone', the slate- or metal-topped bench on which compositors assemble the metal type. Metal replaced stone decades ago, but 'stone' survived. Now photocomposition is replacing typesetting. Several sections of the paper are made up on paste-up boards, which resemble easels. I no longer talk of 'being on the stone'. But like the Lord (to misquote Job), computer technology − any technology − hath given as well as taken away. I intend later to give examples of how it is enriching the language (see REDUNDANT).

26 JULY 1981

CONTROVERSY

− that is what my piece on pejoratives (see PUT-DOWNS) landed me in. The arguments arose not about the words I was dealing with, poetaster and *pace*, but about 'pejorative' itself: is the stress on 'pe-' or '-jor-'? Colleagues were divided, but not as fiercely as they were over the word this piece starts with. 'There's no argument about it, it's "con*trov*ersy"', said one lot. 'There's no argument about it', said another, 'it's "*controv*ersy".' Feelings ran high.

As for the pronunciation of 'pejorative', Webster's New Collegiate and Collins have the stress on '-jor-' first and 'pe-' second, the Concise Oxford vice versa; the Longman Dictionary of Contemporary English has it on '-jor-' only. There is more agreement on 'controversy': Webster has the stress on 'cont-' only, the others on 'cont-' first.

It's all to do with 'recessive accent', the tendency in English to place the stress early in the word. As the arguments among my colleagues (and differences in the dictionaries) indicate, the 'recessivists' do not have it entirely their way.

19 JULY 1981

‿ORRECT.' Mr Robert A. Crawford, of Ruislip, in Middlesex, writes: 'If a person uses a phrase such as "It is one of those things that . . ." it is odds-on that the sentence will not be correctly completed.'

He quotes Radio 4's 'Today' on 10 November: 'One of those things that has to be dealt with . . .' (Sir Geoffrey Howe). There follows: *The Observer*, 7 August: 'One of those small-hour shows that offers . . .' (Paul Ferris); *The Observer*, 23 October: '. . . one of the rare businessmen who actually likes journalists' (Michael Davie); *The Observer*, 30 October: 'Herbert Morrison . . . is one of the few men who comes out of the affair with some credit' (A. J. P. Taylor); *The Observer*, 30 October: 'One of the things that has happened to Kenneally . . .' (Michael Davie).

The point is that all those singular verbs − '*has* to be dealt with', 'offers', etc. − should be plural. (*The Observer* is not alone: Mr Crawford mentions a leading article − on education − in *The Times* as well as a letter from a headmaster.)

I am contrite on behalf of my colleagues and myself − I had to read the letter twice before the penny dropped. But it occurs to me that if writers as good as Messrs Davie, Ferris and Taylor can make this mistake, may it not be an example of changing usage?

Originally 'conservancy', from the Latin *conservatio*, conservation, was spelt conservacy. 'Internecine', like its Latin source, *internecinus*, was defined as destructive. Dr Johnson, in his Dictionary of the English Language (1755), apparently for no good reason introduced an 'n' into the first and defined the second as *mutually* destructive.

4 DECEMBER 1983

Letters from readers who disagreed with Mr Crawford were many and confident. (Mr Goran Kjellmer, of the English Institute at Goteborg University, in Sweden, sent me an offprint of a twenty-page article that had originally appeared in the English-language learned journal *Anglia*, which is published in Germany.) Somewhat shaken, I took the matter to a grammatical court of appeal: Professor Randolph Quirk, Vice-Chancellor of London University and co-author of *A Grammar of Contemporary English*, and Dr Robert Burchfield, Chief Editor of the Oxford English Dictionaries, who is shortly to revise Fowler.

Professor Quirk wrote: 'You are one of the chaps who is/are always raising interesting and difficult questions. Both can be justified. Everything depends on whether the focus is on the underlying generality or on the uniqueness. In, "Charlatanry is one of the many words in English that *are* of French origin", *are* has as its subject the plural *words*, because our attention is on the many words taken from French (and "charlatanry" is but one example). Notice, with transposition, "Of the many words in English that *are* of French origin, 'charlatanry' is one."

'In, "Charlatanry is one of the common vices that *is* particularly contemptible", *is* has as its subject the singular *one*, because our focus is on the particular vice of charlatanry. Again, notice the transposition, "Of the common vice, charlatanry is one that *is* particularly contemptible." '

Dr Burchfield wrote: 'In, "One of the things that − − − − to be dealt with", normal grammatical rules require the dashes to be filled by *have*, not *has*: antecedents should not be disregarded in the printed word. In speech, however, number attraction sometimes leads people to use the type, "One of the x's that" followed by a singular verb, and such attraction can go unremarked even by fastidious speakers. A different kind of number attraction is shown in the (erroneous) type, "One in five are deaf" (correctly *is*).' All of which is why *I* shall continue to write 'correct' and 'incorrect' when discussing usage.

4 MARCH 1984

COSMETIC.

A substance used to enhance one's looks; there is cosmetic surgery; a cosmetic change is superficial rather than one that goes to the heart of the matter − all rather ordinary, even, in the last sense, faintly pejorative. But the word 'cosmetic' has associations with one of the most tremendous concepts ever formulated: the music of the spheres.

It comes from the Greek *kosmos*. My abridged Greek lexicon gives the first meaning as order, then good order, then an ornament, then 'the world, or universe, from its perfect *arrangement.*' It was Pythagoras (*fl.* 540–510 BC) who first used it in that last sense. Pythagoras believed in metampsychosis, or transmigration of souls; he was also one of the great pioneers in mathematics — he discovered the mathematical ratios that determine the principal intervals between musical notes — and astronomy. He maintained that the bodies of the Universe, including Earth, were spheres, revolving around the central body and giving out musical tones that produced an harmonious chord, though one that was not, alas, audible to mankind.

Sir Thomas Browne wrote in *Religio Medici* (1642): 'For there is a music wherever there is a harmony, order of proportion; and thus far we may maintain the music of the spheres; for those well ordered motions, and regular paces, though they give no sound unto the ear, yet to the understanding they strike a note most full of harmony.'

11 NOVEMBER 1979

COUP. The president of troubled El Salvador, José Napoleon Duarte, talking about rumours of a *coup d'état* last month, was quoted in *The Times* as saying, 'The extreme Right is always eager to coup.' Eyebrows were raised, but several dictionaries show the word as verb as well as noun: to strike or overturn. Scots usage, admittedly, but it does seem to back the president.

Similarly the US Secretary of State, Alexander Haig, was taken to task by the columnist William Safire (author of *Safire's Political Dictionary*) for saying, in reply to a question about 'immorality in high places', 'Not as you contexted it, Senator.' But again, what's wrong? Using nouns as verbs is as old as the language. Take 'harbour'. The earliest examples for both the verb and the noun are dated 1150.

The one I want to see is 'to intellect', by which I mean to understand by reasoning. I can't find it in any dictionary, whereas 'to intuit', to understand without reasoning, appears in them all.

19 APRIL 1981

COWBOY.

Mr John Parker MP has written to ask how the present derogatory sense of 'cowboy' developed from the 'heroes of the Red Indian v. cowboy battles of the nineteenth century'. A poignant question. There was a time when the cowboy, to me, epitomised courage, chivalry, endurance – everything a small boy brought up on Westerns aspired to. Nowadays I associate the word with 'motorway': in Volume I of A Supplement to the Oxford English Dictionary the first example of 'cowboy' in the sense of reckless driver is dated 1942; it comes from the US journal *American Speech*. Elaine Dundy, in *The Dud Avocado*, (1958) writes: 'One of those drugstore-cowboy motoring types, just past their first juvenile delinquency.' In 1964, the year before Ian Smith announced UDI, the *Economist* referred to the 'Front, which is called the "cowboy" government by its Rhodesian opponents'.

But perhaps cowboys in real life were not as perfect as I used to think. 'The cowboy', says the main OED, 'does his work on horseback and leads a rough life, which tends to make him rough and wild in character.' That entry was prepared for publication in 1893. Almost a century earlier, in the American Revolutionary War, colonists who remained loyal to Great Britain were called Tories. 'Cowboy', according to another OED example, was 'a contemptuous appellation applied to some of the tory partisans of Westchester Co., New York . . . who were exceedingly barbarous to their opponents who favored the American cause.'

10 APRIL 1983

DAFFODIL:

common English name for the genus Narcissus, which belongs to the Amaryllis family. Even that flat horti-culturist definition has beguiling echoes: Narcissus, the Grecian lad who 'looked into a forest well and never looked away again' (A. E. Housman); Milton's 'To sport with Amaryllis in the shade.' But 'daffodil' is the interesting one.

In Greek legend the asphodel is 'the most famous of the plants connected with the underworld. Homer describes it as covering the great meadow, the haunt of the dead' (Britannica). In the 1500s the word 'affodil,' the English version of 'asphodel', was applied, by confusion, to a species of

Narcissus; at about the same time 'affodil' acquired the 'd'. Eventually ' "Affodil" was confined to *Asphodelus* and "Daffodil" to *Narcissus*' (OED).

Daffodils have inspired some fine verse: Kipling's 'This season's Daffodil,/She never hears,/What change, what chance, what chill,/Cut down last year's;/But with bold countenance,/ And knowledge small,/Esteems her seven days' continuance,/ To be perpetual'; Wordsworth's '. . . a crowd,/A host of golden daffodils'; Shakespeare's '. . . daffodils,/That come before the swallow dares, and take/The winds of March with beauty' – consider the power and precision of that word 'take'. And Herrick, 'Faire Daffadills, we weep to see', of course, but even more haunting, his 'Divination by a Daffadill':

> When a Daffadill I see,
> Hanging down his head t'wards me;
> Guess I may, what I must be:
> First, I shall decline my head;
> Secondly, I shall be dead;
> Lastly, safely buryed.

13 MARCH 1983

DECUS ET TUTAMEN, the Latin inscription round the edge of the new £1 coin, is puzzling people. It is a quotation from Book V of Vergil's Aeneid, and refers to the prize Aeneas gave one of his ship's captains for coming second in a race: 'A coat of mail with polished links of triple gold, a glory and a defence' (*decus et tutamen*; Loeb translation). Mr E. Lloyd-Jones, of Llanfairfechan, comments: 'To describe a coat of mail as an ornament and a means of defence may be quite appropriate, but the description hardly fits the new coin. Some might consider it an ornament, but I am not sure about its defensive qualities.'

While quite liking the coin – Mr Lloyd-Jones's tone suggests that he doesn't – I too did not see the point of the inscription, so I consulted the Royal Mint. Inscriptions, I was told, commonly appeared on early coins to discourage clipping. They varied from coin to coin and period to period. *Decus et tutamen* appeared on coins minted in 1663, under Charles II, notably the gold five-guinea piece and the silver crown and half-crown.

21

Much of this was reported last month when the coin was issued. What I did not take in was that it was the *inscription itself* that constituted 'an ornament and a safeguard' (as the mint translation has it). Against clipping? Rather against forgery. Certainly it is an ornament. The lettering, in italic upper-case, is most elegant, as is the Llantrisant Cross, which also appears on the edge. In 1971 the Mint moved from the Tower of London to Llantrisant, in mid-Glamorgan. For the first time a coin of the realm bears a mark representing the Mint in Wales.

29 MAY 1983

DINNER/SUPPER.

A barrister sits down with his wife in the evening to: soup and a roast with vegetables (cooked by her); cheese and fruit; modest wine; coffee. Dinner or supper? In *Nicholas Nickleby* Newman Noggs grumbles when he is kept working till 'five to three' that his correct dinner time is two and that he had his breakfast at eight. So, roughly, it would have been for most people, upper class, middle or low (though many of the last would have been grateful for one square meal a day, let alone two or three).

Even then, however, we learn from Jane Austen and others, dinner was getting late for the well-to-do; indeed in *Nicholas Nickleby* the wicked Sir Mulberry Hawk has a dinner that goes on till nearly midnight. By the end of the century it was being eaten, 'by the professional and fashionable classes, usually in the evening' – OED, definition prepared for publication in 1898. Nowadays it is more complicated than ever: a character in Barbara Pym's *Some Tame Gazelle* (1950) says of a meal at the vicarage, 'We had supper . . . well, dinner really, because there was soup, though I *think* it was tinned.'

So, what about that barrister and his wife? It is all rather unimportant, but my guess is that, unless there were formally invited guests, it would have been supper.

28 FEBRUARY 1982

DISCREET/DISCRETE.

Recently I came across the phrase 'discrete [historical] facts'. It made no sense: what I had read was 'discreet' (as in 'discreet silence') instead of 'discrete' meaning separate, as in Planck's Quantum Theory of physics, according to which energy is emitted in radiation in discrete amounts (see QUANTUM JUMP). The big Oxford, besides explaining the difference between the two words, revealed that one was a doublet of the other.

A doublet is one of two words different in sense and spelling but derived from the same source, in this case the Latin *discretus*, past participle of *discernere*, to separate, but also, by transference, to distinguish or discern − whence discretion. Other doublets are: balm/balsam, frail/fragile, ratio/reason, shirt/skirt. I like clock and cloak.

Clock originally meant bell: 'The clockes of Saynt Steuen . . . had a merueylous sweteness in theyr sowne' (Caxton's *Golden Legend*, 1483); compare the German *Glocke* and French *cloche*. Cloak, says the OED, comes from the medieval Latin *cloca*, 'cape worn by horsemen and travellers, the same word as *cloche*, so called from its shape. Cloak is thus a doublet of clock.'

7 MARCH 1982

DISMAL, besides its atmosphere of gloom, has a fascinating derivation. It comes from the Latin *dies mali*, the two evil, or unlucky, days a month in the medieval calendar. The Oxford English Dictionary lists them: 1, 25 Jan; 4, 26 Feb; 1, 28 March; 10, 20 April; 3, 25 May; 10, 16 June; 13, 22 July; 1, 30 Aug; 3, 21 Sept; 3, 22 Oct; 5, 28 Nov; 7, 22 Dec. The OED adds that they were also called 'Egyptian days' because they were first 'computed by Egyptian astrologers, though some medieval writers connected them with the plagues of ancient Egypt . . . Some, still more fancifully, connected them with "Egyptian" darkness.'

Then there is 'disaster', from 'dis-' (expressing a negative) and the French *astre*, a star − ill-starred. The first definition in the OED is 'an unfavourable aspect of a star or planet; "an obnoxious planet" (obs).'

And 'debacle', for me the most graphic of all, from the French *débâcler*, to unbar. The OED's first definition is 'a break-up of ice in a river', thence, 'a sudden breaking up or downfall; a confused rout or stampede'. I never see the word in this more usual, figurative sense (e.g. the sudden collapse of a regime, or rout of an army) without also seeing in the mind's eye one of those Russian or North American rivers in the spring thaw, the terrifying sweep of water carrying all before it — trees, rocks, any living creature unfortunate (ill-starred?) enough to be caught up in it.

28 JUNE 1981

EMBUGGERANCE.

The word appeared in the *Guardian* on 26 January in John Ezard's article on soaring Falklands expenditure, including the £130 000 prefabs first reported in *The Observer*. At first I thought it might be one of those lovely *Grauniad* misprints which, rather to my regret, seem to have disappeared. But it occurred twice, once in the plural, so I asked Mr Ezard for its origin. 'Embuggerance', he replied, 'which I've heard used by Royal Engineers officers in the Falklands and in London, is, as far as I can make out, a set of circumstances due partly to unavoidable natural problems, partly to human cock-ups. The speaker is responsible for neither, but expects to find himself carrying the can. Example: a tool wears out unexpectedly quickly on Falklands quartzite which, though no one in London realised it, is unusually abrasive. London is asked for a suitable tool, but neglects to order it quickly enough to catch any of the following week's airbridge flights. This puts the job a week behind schedule. Then an inexperienced squaddie misuses the new tool, breaks it, and the whole process starts again. All this constitutes an embuggerance for the officer in charge who has to run around — "like a headless chicken" — trying to remedy things.'

A parallel construction based on another obscenity is 'snafu,' explained in most dictionaries as *s*ituation *n*ormal *a*ll *f*ucked (or *f*ouled) *u*p; the Concise Oxford gives only '*f*ouled'. It is described as US slang. Perhaps, but in the Second World War the British Army had OMFU and IMFU, in which the first two letters respectively were 'ordinary military' (for such situations as subaltern level) and 'imperial military' (general officer level).

19 FEBRUARY 1984

24

Little Barford, Huntingdon

SIR, *My attention has been drawn to the appearance of the word 'embuggerance' in your columns, page 52, 19 February. About twenty years ago the Central Electricity Board constructed a power line which went through my farm. The wayleave officer who dealt with compensation for damage to crops, fences etc used this word to cover items of general inconvenience not included under specific headings, and it has been part of my vocabulary since that time.*

Yours faithfully

M. WOLSTENHOLME

Winchester

SIR, *The word 'embuggerance' describes a situation that, as an electronic engineer, I know only too well. Another useful acronym like 'acronym' is 'hobart': highly organised buggering about regardless of time.*

Yours faithfully
NIGEL ELLIS

ÉMIGRÉ/IMMIGRANT. Professor Randolph Quirk has given me these thoughts on New Britons: 'Reflecting both the etymology in respect of prefixes and the difference in prestige between the relatively OK French word and the coldly official-sounding English one, "e" reflects on where the person has come from, "i" the place where the person has fetched up. Thus, one is more likely to hear "I am an emigré", "He is an immigrant". The "e" might well go on with tall stories of the heroism of his escape and the horrors of the regime he left behind. The "i" would be expected to think in terms of what he was hoping to get out of the place he had got into.

'In consequence of all this, we develop the ethos that "e's" deserve our respect (and they get it, especially as respect costs so little); while "i's" deserve our support, sympathy, and ("Let's face it", says the tight-lipped liberal) our charity: in fact, they don't get much.

'One will speak with pride in NW11 or Eastbourne of having emigrés (from wherever) as one's neighbours; in Brixton,

Lewisham, Southall (or Bradford or Bristol) it's a different story.'

ENVIOUS/JEALOUS.

Two words used synonymously more often than not. However, as Webster's Eighth New Collegiate Dictionary (1977) says, although they share the sense of begrudging another possession of something, 'these words are not close synonyms and can rarely be used without loss of precision or alteration of emphasis'.

Envy implies desire for something not one's own. Jealousy has to do with what one regards as one's own. Mr A. may envy Mr B. his wife; Mr B. would be jealous if his wife had an affair with Mr A. ('Mrs', 'her' and 'husband' can be substituted at will.) Jealousy in that sense is the 'green-eyed monster' of *Othello*. It also has a non-derogatory sense: 'Proud of their calling, conscious of their duty, jealous of their honour' (Galsworthy). Or, in that tremendous Commandment (Exodus XX 3:5): 'Thou shalt have no other gods before me . . . for I the Lord thy God am a jealous God.'

In its 'envious' entry, the big two-volume Webster's Third New International (1961) notes that the word 'is likely to suggest a grudging of another's possessions and accomplishments, a spiteful desiring of their loss, or, most frequently, a malicious or cankerous coveting of them ("his successes were so repeated that no wonder the envious and the vanquished spoke sometimes with bitterness regarding them" − W. M. Thackeray). "Jealous" may suggest distrustful, suspicious, angry or malcontent intolerance of anyone else's coming to possess what is viewed as belonging to or befitting oneself . . . ("I know that religion, science and art are all jealous of each other because each of them claims, in a sense, to cover the whole field, that is, to interpret all experience from its own point of view" − W. R. Inge) . . .'

Webster's Seventh New Collegiate has a much shortened but still useful version of that note. The Eighth has the admirably cogent note quoted in my piece above. The Ninth, which came out in 1983 (see WEBSTER'S), has, regrettably, no note at all.

EPONYM, from the Greek *epi*, upon, and *onoma*, name. 'One who gives his name to a people, place or institution.'

That is the OED's first definition: 'Pelops is the eponym of the Peloponnesus' (1846). Constantine I is the eponym of Constantinople. Less grand is 'wellington', which has come somewhat down-market since the great duke's day. In *Nicholas Nickleby* (with its eponymous hero) Dickens wrote of 'grey mixture pantaloons, and Wellington boots drawn over them'. All of Shakespeare's histories and tragedies, 23 of his 36 plays, are eponymously titled.

A Dictionary of Eponyms, by Cyril Beeching (Clive Bingley), originally published in 1978, came out last week in a revised, enlarged edition. Opening it at random I read that 'Laszlo Biro was a Hungarian journalist who in 1938 invented the first practical ball-point pen.' He neglected to take out a patent and other men grew rich instead, but 'the ball-point pen is still commonly referred to as a Biro, in the same way that we speak of . . . vacuum cleaners as "Hoovers" (qv).'

Under 'Hoover' I read that J. Murray Spangler, a department store caretaker in Ohio, sold the rights to the new type of vacuum cleaner he had constructed to W. H. Hoover (1849–1935), a businessman. In 1908 'the Hoover Suction Sweeper Company produced the first "Hoover," selling at $70'. Had he kept the rights we might now be speaking 'of "spangling" or "spanglering," instead of hoovering the carpet'.

From another random dip I learnt that the original Daring Young Man on the Flying Trapeze was Jules Léotard (1842–70 – he died of smallpox), a French trapeze artist 'who wore a skin-tight garment during his act'. The book is made for browsing.

31 JULY 1983

ESCALATE. I first met the word in the late 1960s when editing an article by, I think, the American columnist Joseph Kraft (no prizes for guessing what he was writing about). Some of my colleagues disliked it. 'Escalators go up', they said. 'What's wrong with "go up" or "rise"?' I argued that the word conveyed the further impression of *scale*, i.e. an increase in scope, or intensity. Most modern dictionaries agree, although

Collins notes that 'it is not yet completely accepted in formal English'.

1 MARCH 1981

Covent Garden WC2

DEAR SIR, I don't agree with John Silverlight. 'Escalate' conveys the idea of built-in motion. You walk up a staircase. The staircase does not lift you. You are the mover. The escalator propels you to its peak. Thus a verbal quarrel can escalate to a (physical) fight. A local conflict can escalate to a major war. The motion is self-contained and inevitable (unless the machinery is stopped).

Yours sincerely

TUDOR GATES

EU AND NON-EU.

In a lecture on fairy stories J. R. R. Tolkien once used a word of his own coinage, 'eucatastrophe': the 'Consolation of the Happy Ending'. In it he was combining the Greek *eu*, good, and *catastrophe*, not in its general sense of disaster but in its literary sense of denouement. Reading the lecture (published by Allen and Unwin as *Tree and Leaf*) at the time of the General Election, it occurred to me that victory – or even a close-run thing – would have been a eucatastrophe for Mr Foot. There was no eucatastrophe, but it set me thinking about other 'eu-' words and their opposites, those beginning with 'dys-', bad.

Some are of ancient and honourable lineage. The OED's first example with 'dysentery' (from the Greek *dysenteros*, afflicted in the bowels), in a work by Wycliffe, is dated 1382. In 1699 John Evelyn wrote of herbs that are eupeptic (*eu* and *peptein*, to digest) 'and promote concoction' (the original sense of which is digestion). Some are eye-glazing. One such reads: 'The idea of achievement was dysfunctional at that time but eufunctional as anticipatory socialisation for the future.' That example, dated 1968, is in the file of the Oxford English Dictionaries. So, I am pleased to say, is this: 'A new word is creeping into the spartan corridors of Whitehall . . . *euphobia*, which, loosely translated, means fear of good news' (*The Observer*, 21 August 1977). It was coined by my friend William Keegan, *The Observer*'s

Economics Editor, over lunch with a Treasury contact.

10 JULY 1983

EXISTENTIAL. Leigh Woods, who previews films in our

TV guide on the back page, recently commended Walter Hill's 'The Street Fighter' as an 'admirably controlled existential fable about a dour bare-knuckled boxer (Charles Bronson) in mid-Depression New Orleans'. He was clearly using 'existential' to imply a philosophical position rather than in its simple sense of pertaining to existence or expressing the fact of existence. Never having really understood existentialist philosophy, I have always been a bit nervous about the word 'existential'. So, since I trust Woods's judgement, and like Bronson's acting, here was a film to watch.

Woods has provided a gloss on his use of 'existential'. 'Too often', he says, 'one can fall back on it when the right word would be "amoral" or "intellectually blank". Here, however, I was trying to match my word to the precision of the director's style. "The Street Fighter" is in the best dramatic tradition of Sartre (best known of the existentialist philosophers) and Camus, in which the protagonist establishes a hierarchy of values through his actions; he is the sum of his deeds. Bronson embodies a personal ethic which makes him (as the Collins definition of "existentialism" has it) a "free agent in a deterministic and seemingly meaningless universe".'

Not only did I enjoy the film. I am no longer frightened of 'existential'.

14 JUNE 1981

EXPERTISE. ' "You'd have to get someone to do an

expertise." Humphrey was betraying his tinge of linguistic pedantry: that was what expertise meant' (C. P. Snow's last novel, *A Coat of Varnish*, 1979). Expert opinion or appraisal is indeed one meaning of the word, but the late Lord Snow was correct in speaking of Humphrey Leigh's pedantry — hardly anyone uses the word in that sense nowadays.

It does not appear in the main body of the Oxford English Dictionary (the D and E articles, or entries, were published between May 1893 and March 1894). The word's first definition in the Supplement published in 1933, when the complete OED at last appeared, is: 'Expert opinion . . . often expressed through the action of submitting a matter to . . . experts', i.e. Humphrey's use. However, the first example, dated 1868, is, 'I have distanced my competitors in expertise' (from what the Dictionary of National Biography describes as the 'daringly romantic' novel *Foul Play* by Charles Reade, author of *The Cloister and the Hearth*). This seems to illustrate the Supplement's second definition, 'The quality or state of being expert; skill or experience in a particular branch of study or sport', the sense in which most people now use the word.

Judging from examples in Volume I of A Supplement to the OED (1972), usage wobbled between the two senses until the 1920s or 1930s; in the 1950s the second became dominant. Among modern desk dictionaries Longman's Dictionary of Contemporary English gives the 'appraisal' sense second, adding 'esp. BrE'. Against that, the American Webster's Eighth New Collegiate has, '1, expert opinion [with no mention of British English] 2, skill in a particular field'.

16 AUGUST 1981

E̲X̲P̲L̲I̲C̲A̲T̲E̲ and 'replicate'. Both these words appeared in a recent issue of *The Observer*. I wondered how the first differed from 'explain' and the second from 'reproduce'. The clue is found in derivation. 'Explain' comes from the Latin *explanare*, to make smooth, 'explicate' from *explicare*, to unfold. OED examples show that both once had their literally translated senses: 'The Horse-Chesnut ['*Chesnut* was till 1820, *chestnut* is, the current form', Shorter Oxford] is . . . ready to explain its leaf', 1684; 'The Rose of Jericho will explicate its flowers contracted', Sir Thomas Brown, 1646. When unfolding something, one's attention is focused on the action rather than on the result, so that 'explicate' has greater intensity than 'explain': the Concise Oxford and Webster's Collegiate bring this out by including among their definitions, 'To develop the implications of'.

So with 'replicate'. Collins defines the related word 'replica' as an 'exact reproduction'. To replicate is not just to reproduce but to reproduce exactly. All those words from *plicare*, to fold or fold together, have a high degree of intensity. Take one of

Webster's definitions of 'implicate': 'To bring into intimate or incriminating connection'.

1 NOVEMBER 1981

A reader whose letter has regrettably gone astray maintains that a 'replica' is 'a reproduction by the original artist'. Apologies are in order but not grovelling ones. The Shorter Oxford's definition reads: 'A copy, duplicate, or reproduction of a work of art; prop., one made by the original artist. **b.** *transf.* A copy, reproduction, facsimile.'

E YAS, I learnt recently, means immature hawk. From the Concise Oxford I also learnt that it was originally 'nyas', from the Latin *nidus*, nest: the hawk was taken from its nest for training; 'for loss of initial "n-" cf adder'.

So to 'adder', a small, venomous snake, originally a 'naddre', the 'n-' having been lost in Middle English (1100s to 1400s) by 'wrong division . . . cf "apron" [from *naperon*, Old French diminutive of *nappe*, table-cloth], "auger" [from 'nave', the hub of a wheel, and Old English *gar*, spear] and "umpire" [from Old French *nonper*, not equal].'

There was a converse process by which, says the OED entry 'N', the 'n-' of 'an' was frequently transferred to a following word beginning with a vowel', e.g. 'naunt' (an aunt) and 'nuncle' (an uncle) — Lear's Fool, 'Nuncle, give me an egg.' Still in use are 'newt', from 'an ewt,' and 'nickname', from 'an eke-name', an also-name. One example, from 'Wyt and Music' (c. 1530), a morality play by John Redford, Master of the Children of St Paul's in the time of Henry VIII, reads: '. . . I shal bete thy narse, now.'

16 OCTOBER 1983

F ACTION. Resisting change in usage, like trying to stop the tide coming in, is a forlorn hope. But sometimes the temptation is too strong, so here is a bit of resistance – against the use of 'faction' to describe a work that mixes fact and fiction, e.g. Thomas Keneally's *Schindler's Ark*. For one thing there is a dismissive quality about 'faction' in that sense, which rules it out for a book as good as Mr Keneally's. For another the word has had an important use in the world of politics.

The Latin *facere*, to do or make, can also mean to side with or against someone. Similarly *factio*, as well as meaning a way of doing something, also means a 'company of adherents or partisans, usually with the odious accessory notion of oligarchical' – Lewis and Short. (Oligarchy: 'government in which a small group exercises control, esp. for corrupt and selfish purposes' – Webster's Collegiate.) 'Faction' retains that 'odious accessory notion': it conveys, says the OED, 'the imputation of mischievous ends'. Militant Tendency is accused of being a faction.

Incidentally, my use in the first paragraph of 'forlorn hope' is itself an example of changing usage. The expression, adapted from the Dutch *verloren hoop*, lost troop, originally meant 'a picked body of men, detached to the front to begin the attack . . . a storming party'. 'Hope against hope' is the OED's third definition and is used in that sense 'with word-play or misapprehension of the etymology'.

27 MARCH 1983

FEISTY. 'By the end he has the punch-drunk feistiness of the great survivor' – Jon Holliday on works by or about the 74-year-old dictator of Albania, Enver Hoxha (pronounced *hodja*), in the 2–15 September issue of the *London Review of Books*. Volume I of A Supplement to the OED (1972) says 'feisty' is US slang and defines it as 'aggressive, excitable, touchy'. Desk dictionaries generally agree – the Collins English Dictionary, with 'frisky, irritable', is typical. (Collins gives the derivation as, 'C19, from dialect *feist, fist*, small dog, related to Old English *fisting*, breaking wind.')

But those definitions do not fit the sense of 'punch-drunk feistiness', which has a note, however reluctant, of approval. This is already apparent in the unabridged American Webster (1961), 'full of nervous energy', and in the OED Supplement example 'He couldn't shake her loose – she hung on his arm, feisty as a terrier' (1968). The note is heard still more strongly in a later example in the Oxford files: 'Brady was remembering what he liked about her. She was . . . a spirited, feisty woman' (1978).

Nowadays feisty means gutsy, or spunky, both of which are defined in dictionaries as courageous. Note the anatomical element in all those words: the derivation of 'gutsy' is obvious; that of 'feisty' has already been mentioned; 'spunk' is a slang word for semen; 'courage' comes from the Latin *cor*, heart.

31 OCTOBER 1982

Tulse Hill School
London, SW2

DEAR MR SILVERLIGHT, *The black British children at this school whose parents are Jamaican have always used 'feisty' to mean 'cheeky' or 'rude'. It is invariably pejorative though sometimes there is an implication of grudging admiration as in 'He's too feisty.' The phrase 'Coming feisty', is a challenge to combat of some sort.*

Although the word in this sense clearly came with the West Indian immigrants of the Fifties, in this community it is now used and understood by both black and white communities. Other Jamaican idioms have been similarly assimilated in recent years,

Yours sincerely,

STEPHEN WILLIAMS,
Senior Housemaster, Turner House

F**LU.** Even if they are not comforted, sufferers from flu may be interested in some stray facts about its etymology. The OED says that as well as the various senses of the English word 'influence', the Italian *influenza* also has the sense — from the notion of 'astral' or 'occult influence' — of 'visitation' on many people at the same time and place of any disease (e.g., *influenza di catarro* or *influenza di febbre scarlatina*). In 1743 the word was 'applied specifically to "the epidemic" (called also *la grippe*) which then raged in Italy . . . for which the Italian word (anglicised in pronunciation) became the English specific name.' The first abbreviation was 'flue': in an example dated 1839 Southey wrote, 'I have had a pretty fair share of the Flue' (the 'the' is still common — Collins notes that it often precedes 'flu'). The first example of 'flu' is dated 1893.

Sufferers can take some comfort from Britannica's comment that 'mortality is commonly low, resulting in most cases from complications such as pneumonia'. However, it has been one of history's great killers. In the first 20 weeks of 1890 'the tale of [its] victims cannot have fallen far from short of 2,800 for London alone' (OED). And in the world-wide epidemic of 1918-19, just after the Great War, more than 20 million people died of it, twice as many as were killed in the war. Nowadays antibiotics are an almost certain defence against the complications.

20 FEBRUARY 1983

FOREIGNISMS. Avoid them, so runs conventional wisdom and quite right too — as a working rule. But there are exceptions: foreign phrases that express a complicated thought more cogently and comprehensively than anything in English. Here are three:

Mutatus mutandis: taking differences of detail into consideration (the literal translation of the Latin is 'the necessary changes having been made'). Example: 'The problems facing a Prime Minister and the head of a great corporation are, *mutatis mutandis*, very similar.'

Papabile: 'Eligible to be, or like to be Pope' (Cassells Italian dictionary) and, by extension, someone in the running for succession as head of a company, political party, what have you. The operative word is 'likely'. Any member of the Sacred College of Cardinals is eligible to be Pope, just as any member of the parliamentary Labour Party is eligible to be party leader, but only four or five members are *papabile*.

Schadenfreude (from the German *Schade*, damage or harm, and *Freude*, joy): pleasure in another's suffering. Someone I know who detests driving and everything to do with cars feels *Schadenfreude* (and is ashamed of doing so) when he reads about accidents. La Rochefoucauld's 'In the misfortunes of our best friends we always find something that does not displease us' is a subtle version. Confucius is credited with 'There is no spectacle more agreeable than to observe an old friend fall from a rooftop.'

25 JANUARY 1982

FULL OF/FILLED WITH.

Facing me at my desk is a print of Dr Martin Joseph Routh (1755–1854) who said: 'You will find it a very good practice always to verify your references, Sir!' Last month, in a profile of the historian E. P. Thompson, I quoted W. B. Yeats's lines

> The best lack all conviction while the worst
> Are full of passionate intensity.

With Dr Routh in mind I *did* verify the reference, but unfortunately, in the second draft, 'full of' became 'filled with'.

It did not go unnoticed. In the article I had described the lines as 'well-worked'. A reader in Dublin cut out the reference, pasted it on a sheet of writing paper, ringed the words 'well-worked' and wrote beside them 'and misquoted'. Another reader responded with thirty-five lines of verse, reprinted below. Besides apologies I offer a note on the difference in meaning between 'full of' and 'filled with' from Mrs Lesley Burnett, who is revising the Shorter Oxford English Dictionary. She writes: ' "Full" is adjective of state. But "filled" is a participial adjective derived from a transitive verb and as such draws attention to the agent. In this instance it implies that someone or something has filled the worst with passionate intensity. "Full of" offers no such explanation of the state of "the worst" and so contributes to the sense of frightening irrationality in the poem.'

10 MAY 1981

Hereford

DEAR JOHN SILVERLIGHT

This ought to be a time to relax.
It's Sunday evening after supper.
Are we filled with meat and vegetables
Or are we full of meat and vegetables?
I could ask my wife how it is with her

The other side of the stove, in her chair,
But she's sewing the eyes into her rabbit.
Is the rabbit filled with acrilan
Or is the rabbit full of acrilan?
How could that white curve of its stomach

So unsettle me when there are pages
Still to be read in today's Observer?
An article is filled with misquotations
Or an article is full of misquotations?
Jones' room at Peterhouse that night

Was filled with E. P. Thompson's presence.
Or was it full of E. P. Thompson's presence?
But when Thompson left his job at Warwick
Friend of mine, Paul Jeremy, decided
Warwick was so empty he must leave too, Paul

Who'd filled his old headmaster with a dread
Of what might happen when the next election
Forced his country even further to the left.
Poor man was full of thoughts of lamp-posts
And the likelihood of being hanged from one.

Being myself perhaps one of the worst
Historians, poets, teachers, I'm uneasy
As to whether I am filled or full
Of passionate intensity. This rabbit,
Her best, won't say one way or the other.

But I'm free to look up the Collected
Poems if I can slide these glass doors
Back across a glut of paperbacks
Stuffed in above and below solid stuff,
Difficult task, with the state I'm in.

R. D. LANCASTER

GENIAL.

Mrs Kathleen Dejardin, of Mulhouse, in eastern France, chides *The Observer* gently for describing someone as 'genial' in an article, 'apparently in the French sense of genius, not a jolly soul'. Originally 'genial' meant pertaining to propagation ('genius' derives from the Greek *gignesthai*, to be born). Then, by extension, came the sense of 'conducive to growth . . . warm, mild', then 'cheering, inspiriting', then '. . . jovial, kindly'. The French *génial*, says the OED, 'characterised by genius, is a new formation after the German *genial, genialisch*'.

The German connection is explained in the 'genius' entry. First comes the classical pagan sense of attendant spirit 'allotted to every person at birth', then 'demon or spiritual being in general', then 'of persons: characteristic disposition', then 'natural ability or capacity'. In the eighteenth century, says a long note, 'probably influenced by association with senses 1 and 2', came the idea that the word 'had an especial fitness to denote that particular kind of intellectual power which . . . seems to arrive at its result in . . . an inexplicable and miraculous manner'. This use, 'which originated in England . . . gave the designation of *Genieperiode* to the epoch in German literature otherwise known as the *Sturm und Drang* [storm and stress] period.'

Last month, Michael Oliver, in the admirable Radio 3 programme 'Music Weekly', quoted an author as writing that Mozart was a child prodigy who became a genius. *'Became* a genius?' Mr Oliver commented. 'When would that have been? Were all the works before that *ungenial*?' Mrs Dejardin says that her children use *génial* for people and things they heartily approve of.

17 APRIL 1983

GENTLE/GENTILE – what is the relationship between them, a reader asks. Both words come from the Latin *gentilis*; beyond that things get complicated. Originally *gentilis* meant 'of the same tribe'. Then it came to be applied to non-Romans, to foreigners, barbarians. Later still Christians applied it to non-Christians, to pagans, or heathens. The sense *not* found in Latin is 'of good family', as in the Romance languages – *gentilhomme, gentilhombre, gentiluomo* – and the English 'gentle': the first OED example in this sense is dated 1225; the first in the sense of mild, or soft, is dated 1555.

'Gentile', on the other hand, acquired a religious, racial connotation. In the Hebrew bible the word *goyyim*, plural of *goy*, nation, was applied to non-Hebrews. In the Vulgate (translation begun in the fourth century) *goyyim* became *gentiles*, whence its meaning, now as in Chaucer's time, of non-Jewish. 'Gentile' also retained its pagan/heathen connotations, making it possible for Kipling, in his great poem 'Recessional', to write of 'Such boastings as the Gentiles [i.e. non-British] use/Or lesser breeds without the Law.'

So there is indeed a relationship between 'gentle' and 'gentile', but a subtle one. Just think of the irony of

Shakespeare's 'Hie thee, gentle Jew' or, 'We all expect a gentle answer, Jew' in *The Merchant of Venice*.

17 OCTOBER 1982

GERIATRIC.

'Hua Kuo-feng was replaced by Teng Hsiao-ping but a number of geriatrics remained, including Marshal Yeh, 85, the official Head of State' − *Spectator*, 18 September, on a reshuffle in the Chinese leadership. 'Geriatric' comes from the Greek *geras* and *iatros*, old age and physician, and has to do with care of the aged. It does not, say purists, mean old person. Yet here we find it in that sense in that highly literate journal, the *Spectator*, in a piece (judging from the initials at the end, A. A. W.) by one of our more literate journalists, Auberon Waugh. So, how long do we go on resisting it, bearing in mind John Ciardi's dictum that those who care about the language have a duty to resist changes they object to (see PURISTS)?

I asked Mrs Lesley Burnett, who is revising the Shorter Oxford English Dictionary, if she would be quoting that usage in the new edition. 'Probably', she replied. This does not mean it has her blessing. Lexicographers do not bless or condemn changes in usage: they record them. What it means is that the writing is on the wall. The new usage is already in Collins (1979). When it appears in the Shorter Oxford most people will have forgotten it was ever controversial.

14 NOVEMBER 1982

Bristol

SIR, *With reference to John Silverlight's article on the acceptance of 'geriatrics' for old people, I wonder if and when this will be followed by 'paediatrics' for children?*

Yours faithfully,
(Miss) LISELOTTE LESCHKE

A fair point, but we have gone beyond the writing on the wall; Belshazzar is already slain. Six months before my article appeared, provoking Miss Leschke's letter, Anthony Powell's *The Strangers All Are Gone* was published. In it he writes of having 'a sudden vision of scenes of riotous carousal on the part of intoxicated geriatrics' in an old people's home.

GRACE. 'Holy Eucharist 8 a.m.', read the notice outside the church. Where had I met that word recently in a very different context? Then I remembered. I had just returned from Greece; the Greek for 'thank you' is *eucharisto* (pronounced *efharistó*); Holy Eucharist, or Communion, is the Church's meal of thanksgiving.

The heart of the word is *charis*, outward grace or beauty in classical Greek. It also means 'grace or favour felt, whether on the part of the doer or the receiver' (Liddell and Scott's Greek–English Lexicon). It was St Paul who took over the word for his new religion: it is used 101 times in his writings, only 51 times in the rest of the New Testament. So I am told by a clergyman, who defines Grace as 'God's uncovenanted, undeserved mercy towards man, shown in Jesus's incarnation, death and resurrection.'

So far so good. But what about Faith, the price we have to pay for Grace, and Free Will? That's where the trouble started: Pelagius (the British monk who was excommunicated for heresy in AD 417) and Calvin are just two of the names that figure in this most thorny of theological questions.

Classical scholars say Christians have robbed the word of its powerful sexual overtones. In the section on *charis* as 'favour', the lexicon has 'esp. in erotic sense', and it quotes the verb *charizomai*, to pleasure someone. (One of these scholars tells me that in ancient Greek usage the pleasurer was always a man; the pleasured could be of either sex.) In mythology Charis is the wife of Hephaestus, or Vulcan. Vulcan's wife is Venus.

11 APRIL 1982

GUNG HO. A colleague on *The Observer* is puzzled by press references during the Falklands fighting to 'gung ho'. He guessed from context that it was a disparaging term for zealous, or enthusiastic – 'the *Guardian* is noticeably less gung ho about the war than the Sun or *Daily Mail*' – but where did it come from? Webster's Eighth New Collegiate says it was the 'motto (interpreted as meaning "work together") of certain US

marine raiders [Carlson's Raiders] in World War II, from the Chinese *kung-ho*, short for . . . "Chinese Industrial Co-operative Society".' Examples in Volume I of A Supplement to the OED include:

'Carlson frequently has what he calls "kung-how" meetings . . . Problems are threshed out and orders explained' − *Times Magazine* (New York), 1942.

'My motto caught on and they began to call themselves the Gung Ho battalion' − Carlson's *Life*, 1943.

'I've always thought of you as being − I don't know, full steam ahead about life. Not gung ho, exactly, but − well, always ready to manage and organise things' − *Accessory*, by M. Lockwood, 1968.

'In those days he was very gung ho for National Socialism and the pan-Germanic grandeur' − *Kessler Legacy*, by R. M. Stern 1967.

'He was one of the most "gung ho" (exceptionally keen to be personally involved in combat) characters I have ever met' − *British GI in Vietnam*, by I. Kemp, 1969.

'Today's grunts [term for US marine infantry] − are noticeably different from those who filled the enthusiastic "Gung-ho" units of a few years back' − *Times* report from Saigon, 1970.

11 JULY 1982

H ACK. My friend and colleague on *The Observer*, Dr Conor Cruise O'Brien asks me to deprecate what he sees as a growing tendency among journalists to describe themselves as 'hacks': 'HACKS AT WAR', *The Listener*, 8 July; 'a mob of jostling hacks', *Spectator*, 10 July'; 'HOW THE HACKS WON THEIR GONGS', *The Times*, 15 July; '*Observer* [or whichever paper is under attack] hacks', *Private Eye passim*. 'What other profession', Dr O'Brien asks, 'regularly refers to itself disparagingly?'

The word, an abbreviation of 'hackney', originally meant 'a horse for ordinary riding, as distinguished from . . . special riding' and, 'a horse let out for hire' − OED, which also quotes a 1721 definition, 'a common hackney Horse, Coach or

Strumpet'. Inexorably this leads to 'a person whose services may be hired for any kind of work . . . a common drudge, esp. a literary drudge . . . a poor writer, a mere scribbler.' There are references to other professions − 'hack attorneys', 'hack preachers' − but not after 1792; in his *Observer* column on 11 July Alan Watkins referred to 'hack politicians'.

It doesn't particularly offend me. There are racing horses and hacking horses. Dr O'Brien is pre-eminently an example of the former (I happen to think that *The Observer* has an unusually high proportion of racing horses, but then I would, wouldn't I). However, there are good hacking horses and bad hacking horses. Since I consider myself a good one (again I would, wouldn't I), I almost take pride in describing myself as a hack: rather like the Old Contemptibles in the Great War.

8 AUGUST 1982

IE/SHE, says the Second Barnhart Dictionary of New English, 'continues to gain in popularity' over other would-be substitutes for 'he or she'. I sympathise with the search for such a word. But what is wrong with 'they' as in 'Someone put their head round my door' (Julian Barnes in this paper, 6 June)? Purists argue that 'they' needs a plural antecedent, but, as Barnhart shows, that did not worry Shakespeare ('Everyone to rest themselves/), Shaw ('It's enough to drive anyone out of their senses') or Scott Fitzgerald ('Nobody likes a mind quicker than their own').

Barnhart II consists of words, with examples of usage, collected from 1973−9 (it is published in New York and appeared in this country last month, distributed by Longman). Barnhart I, covering 1963−72, explains that 'the order of the quotations is not necessarily chronological and no attempt is made to give the earliest quotation available. The emphasis is placed instead on the utility of the quotations.'

The OED does aim at tracing 'first uses'. The first example of SALT, for instance, in Volume III of the Supplement, from Mrs L. B. Johnson's 'White House Diary' (1968), is, 'When . . . the talks would start we do not know. They are being referred to as Strategic Arms Limitation Talks (SALT).' Barnhart II, with two examples of SALT dated 1976, gives 1972 as 'the year of its earliest appearance in our files or in other sources as far as the editors could ascertain', which I find confusing. However,

Barnhart is both helpful and entertaining, and I look forward to using it.

W fertig

2 JANUARY 1983

HOLISTIC.

A fashionable word, especially in connection with medicine. Readers of *The Observer* are asking about it. The word 'holism', from the Greek *holos*, whole, was coined by Jan Christiaan Smuts in *Holism and Evolution* (Macmillan, 1926), in which he wrote that 'both matter and life consist of unit structures whose ordered grouping produces natural wholes'. The book ends: 'The rise and self-perfection of wholes in the Whole is the slow but unerring process and goal of this Holistic universe.' This, like Teilhard de Chardin's theory that man is 'evolving, mentally and socially, towards a final spiritual unity' (Britannica), strikes me as rather difficult to demonstrate scientifically. But the holistic concept is useful. A human being, any animal, is 'more than the sum of its parts' (Smuts's phrase). Janet Watts, writing in *The Observer* on 18 September, quoted the chairman of the British Holistic Medical Association as saying that 'the essence of the holistic approach is that it treats the whole person, body, mind and spirit'.

'Whole' comes from the Old English *hal*, akin to the Old High German *heil*, healthy, unhurt ('the "wh" first appears in the 15th century' – OED). The Greek *holis* comes, with linguistic twists, from the Sanskrit *sarva*, whole, entire, complete, but Mr Christopher Reynolds, of the School of Oriental and African Studies, quotes the Sanskrit Dictionary as saying 'there is no connection between *sarva* and the English "whole"'. The chiming of 'whole' and *holis* in sound and sense is thus a linguistic coincidence. Mr Reynolds gave me another such coincidence. The Persian for bad is *bad*. Again there is no linguistic connection.

20 NOVEMBER 1983

HUNTER.

In his youth the late Lord Dilhorne (formerly Sir Reginald Manningham-Buller), according to his *Times* obituary, was an enthusiastic huntsman. Enthusiastic, perhaps, but almost certainly not a huntsman, the man 'whose business it is

42

to take charge of the hounds' (OED). But if not huntsman, what? Not hunter which, to people who hunt, is a breed of horse. There are circumlocutions – 'rider to hounds', 'fox-hunting man' – but these aren't really satisfactory, especially the second: what about women who hunt?

The same 'lexicographical gap' (I get the expression from my friend Professor Randolph Quirk) is met in another blood sport. As with fox-hunting, someone who shoots at birds is not, in Britain, a hunter although that is the word used in the United States and, in translation, other countries: *chasseur, cacciatore, cazador, jäger*. One is reluctant, Professor Quirk observed, to put names to sacred things. I don't think he was being entirely jocular.

8 MARCH 1981

Belfast

Surely the word for one who shoots birds is fowler?
M. GRANT CORMACK

I DO/I WILL. Vera Thompson, of Parbold, in Lancashire, commenting on the title of Professor Eysenck's recent book '*I Do': Your Guide to a Happy Marriage*, writes: 'The responses in a Christian marriage in this country are "I will", not "I do". "I will" is a vow, "I do" is not. Have you any idea why the "I do" idea is so widespread? It appears in plays, books and popular entertainment. On the wedding day of the Prince and Princess of Wales the *Daily Telegraph* printed a whole-page poem by Spike Milligan in which he said "I do" several times.'

My first thought was that the slip – if slip it was – might be a subconscious echo of the Order of Confirmation, in which 'I do' is the response to the bishop's question, 'Do ye renew the solemn promise and vow that was made [by your Godparents] at your Baptism?' Then I wondered, what do people say in register offices?

The General Register Office (Births, Deaths and Marriages) says there are two declarations: 'I do solemnly declare that I know of no lawful impediment why I, so-and-so, may not be joined in matrimony to so-and-so' and, 'I call upon these present here to witness that I, so-and-so, do take thee, so-and-

43

so, to be my lawful wedded wife/husband.'

Here, possibly, is the explanation Vera Thompson is seeking.

10 JULY 1983

Mrs M. M. Coats, of Southampton, and two clergymen, Mr Roger Parsons (Methodist, in Brentwood, Essex) and Mr G. R. Steele (Anglican, in South Glamorgan), agree on an explanation of the increasing use of 'I do' rather than 'I will' to symbolise marriage. It is the influence of American films in which, almost invariably, the question put to a couple at a wedding is 'Do you, so-and-so, take this woman/man etc.' Father Fred Howard, of the Episcopal Church Centre, New York, confirms that while he would ask '*Will* you', his civil counterpart, usually a judge, would ask '*Do* you.' Q.E.D.

24 JULY 1983

I/ME. A reader in Harpenden, Herts, has been monitoring the BBC for examples of the 'nob's pronoun' as in 'between you and I'. His list includes: 'From you and I' — David Dimbleby; 'That gives she and her partner match point' — Dan Maskell; 'My father brought my sister and I back from India' — Wendy Craig; 'Everything comes to he who waits' — Russell Harty (although he immediately corrected himself); 'So, from Arthur Negus and I, goodbye' — Angela Rippon.

All this, says Fowler (second edition, 1968), 'is a piece of false grammar which, though often heard, is not sanctioned . . . even in colloquial usage'. Not just 'often heard'. Dr Robert Burchfield, Chief Editor of the Oxford English Dictionary, says it is 'racing away into general, even educated use'. People who worry about the state of the language see it as just one more example of decline. I am not so sure. It goes back a long way — Fowler speaks of its 'distinguished history' and cites Shakespeare ('All debts are cleared between you and I'), Pepys ('Wagers lost between him and I') and Dickens ('Leave Nell and I to toil and work'). (Fowler also has an example of the 'yob's pronoun': 'Mrs Forster and me are such friends' — Lydia Bennet (who else) in *Pride and Prejudice*.)

Dr Burchfield blames it on the decreasing teaching in schools of languages with inflected pronouns, the French *je, me* and the like. But why did it ever start? My pet theory is — as the 'distinguished history' suggests — that the English have always been uneasy about some uses of 'I': what we need is the equivalent of *moi*. '*C'est moi*' in reply to '*Qui est là?*' sounds right: 'It's I' doesn't. Some days ago several of us agonised over the phrase 'older than I'. In the end we made it — mistakenly, as we now agree — 'older than me'. Bruno Bettelheim, in his interesting and important *Freud and Man's Soul* (Chatto and Windus), attacks the translation of Freud's *das Ich* as 'the ego'. One sees what he means, but the translators had a problem: one doesn't speak of 'the I'. 'I' is an awkward word.

7 AUGUST 1983

Most of the many letters provoked by I/ME (almost as many as were provoked by LOO) come down on me for finding difficulty with such phrases as 'older than I'. There are exceptions. Mr Sam Deering, who teaches English to immigrant children at a Wembley comprehensive after living in Italy for many years (in the Second World War he fought with Italians against the Germans), writes: 'Surely there are older precedents — "methinks [dates of OED quotations range from 888 (King Alfred) to 1878], "meseems" [1400—1876], "it likes me", "it likes me not" [971—1850]. It was perhaps Latinisation which drove these expressions out, whereas you will still find them in the so-called Latin languages.

'A bad Italian grammar will teach you to say *egli é* for the third person singular. A good one will teach you to say what is universally used — *lui é*, although *lui* is normally a dative. The feminine is no different: *lei* and *Lei* (the second used as a formal second person singular; note the similarity between the Italian and German) are invariably used as nominatives though properly dative; *essa* and *ella* are relegated to the pedant's lumber room.

'*Mi* (accusative) and *me* (dative) are used as nominatives only in dialect, but very widely so, and to describe Venetian, Meneghino [city of Milan], Romanesco or Neapolitan as dialects is somewhat stretching things, for they and many more local ones are literary and commercial languages.

'And speaking of dialects, if we turn to English, in my native dialect of the Devon—Somerset border, *Er give it tü I* was once the common way of rendering "He gave it to me". Indeed, dialect grammars are a rich source for speculation on what

45

standard English might have been, as Italian dialects are, in the hypothesis of *Vita Nova* having emanated from any but the Florentine speaker Dante.

'It is very difficult to pin these English dialects down, for they vary so greatly within a constricted area. There was a conjugation in NW Somerset which ran *oi be, tha bis, er be/us be, you be, they be*. No more than twenty miles to the south it ran *oim, heem, sheem, sheem/weem, youm, theym*, where *sheem* was both feminine and neuter. Even quite locally *sheem* might be replaced by *erm*. I feel that quite often the apparent grammatical solecism is owed to the great changes in the morphology of pronouns over the centuries. What was the Wessex *er* (now, alas, disappearing)? And why is *us* a nominative in Wessex and possessive in Yorkshire?

'I leave you with a memorable sentence uttered in the 1920s by my grandfather's old housekeeper, then in her seventies; she lived to be ninety-eight. We had arrived late at Tiverton Station and the connection to Tiverton Junction had probably gone. She said, "Weem tü laït for she unless er be laït tü." '

Dr Harold Somers, of the Manchester University Institute of Science and Technology, writes that the long tradition of using Latin and Greek as a model in English grammar teaching 'is now regarded by linguists as quite inappropriate, since English did not develop from other language (it merely borrowed a lot of vocabulary which it strings together using German syntax). In Latin the verb "to be" takes a nominative: therefore, said the prescriptive grammarians, so should the English "to be". Phrases like "It is I who . . ." must be *learnt* by most speakers, since the more natural "me" — for which linguists use the term disjunctive pronoun — is branded as uneducated.' Seeds of uncertainty are sown, leading to such things as the nob's — and yob's — pronoun.

'Modern linguists tend to avoid prescription and pro-scription, that is making pronouncements about what is correct or incorrect, preferring simply description, that is saying what is found in the language without making any value judgments. This being the case, it is not our job to suggest the reinstatement of "me" as the correct form of the disjunctive pronoun. The best we can do is state the facts, which are that the historically more natural accusative has been superseded in so-called educated speech by the nominative (though I'm not sure that this is entirely so: do people say "It is we" or "It is us"?), though it still remains in colloquial usage. And in years to come we may have to report that the change from accusative to nominative is complete if phrases like "between you and I" become accepted as correct.

'Mr Silverlight suggests that speakers are uneasy about the use of "I", and need an equivalent of *moi*: we did have one — "me" — but have been made to feel uneasy about that too! The unease stems from a conflict between what is linguistically and historically natural and what we have been *told* is correct.'

Professor John Honey, Head of the School of Education, Leicester Polytechnic, has sent me a blockbusting collection of these pronouns in a copy of a handout he uses when 'giving a pet lecture to foreign audiences on "The Changing English Language". I use it to illustrate my contention that the language is changing in the direction of caselessness for pronouns (as for nouns etc already).'

Here are some of Professor Honey's fifty-seven examples: '. . . but, for we western countries' — Malcolm Muggeridge; 'It is for we in chapel this evening' — Dr Ernest Wilson, Oriel Professor of the Interpretation of Holy Scripture, Oxford University; 'They [bats] are warm-blooded creatures just like you or I' — Dr David Bellamy; 'for we who remain' — Mrs Margaret Thatcher; 'I don't think there's any major difference between him and I' — Dr David Owen; 'driving a wedge between we *goys* and our many deeply loved Jewish friends' — Dr Desmond Flower, former chairman of Cassells; 'Why should the unions expect you and I to pay for support of strikers' families?' — Mr Paul Channon, MP; 'From a certain Mrs Mary Whitehouse, but not from she alone' — Professor Brian Coombridge, University of London Extra-Mural Studies; 'So I said, "Madam, if you cannot respect me as Her Majesty's inspector, you should at least show respect for she whom I represent" ' — senior HMI, describing to a junior colleague an altercation with a recalcitrant teacher; 'First of all they gave my wife and I two forms apiece to fill in' — Dan Jacobson; 'People are always asking how two lunatics like Judy and I have such normal kids' — Thomas Kenneally.

And Vera Thompson, of Parbold, in Lancashire, wonders 'if the awkwardness of "I" is one of the reasons royals use "one" '. I think this is more due to a wish not to sound egotistical, but it is an interesting idea.

28 AUGUST 1983

47

IMPORTANT(LY). Dr Robert Burchfield, in *The Spoken Word: a BBC Guide* (see SPOKEN WORD), writes that with the possible exception of 'disinterested' in the sense of 'uninterested', the use of 'hopefully' in the sense of 'it is hoped' attracted more unfavourable comment from listeners than any other item in his list of words that cause offence. Since I like a quiet life I would not use 'hopefully' in that sense, but it does not really bother me. As Dr Burchfield says, other 'sentence adverbs', such as 'thankfully', are not objected to, especially 'important(ly)' in the phrase 'more important(ly)'.

Personally I object to 'more importantly'. Except to make it more portentous, I cannot see what '-ly' adds to 'more important' — Dr Burchfield says both are equally common and correct'.

Strangely, 'more significant' does not work in this sense; one needs the '-ly'. I suppose it is another instance of the capriciousness noted by Dr Johnson in the way language is conducted.

14 FEBRUARY 1982

IN/AT. Mr David Roberts, of Long Ashton, near Bristol, points out that on 10 April *The Observer* referred to the Department of the Environment's 'wildlife statistics centre at Bristol'. 'I would have expected "in" ', he writes. 'If, when away from home, I am asked where I live, I reply, "in Bristol." If asked in which part, I often reply, "at Long Ashton" (not strictly within the City of Bristol). This leads me to consider whether we differentiate according to the size of the place, or at least the relative size. We do seem to say "at" when speaking of a town as a shorthand for an institution in it: as a student I used to say I was "at Bristol"; MPs are "at Westminster"; people may get on or off a train "at Leeds."

'London never seems to be linked with "at." "He lived at London" doesn't sound right. Nor does "there was an accident on the M4 at London," whereas "on the M4 at Hammersmith" seems acceptable. (On 10 April too *The Observer* reported a fatal road accident "on the M32 at Bristol".)

'Is all this because "at" pinpoints an exact location in the context of the wider area in which it is situated? To me Bristol is a large area. Possibly to a (parochial?) London journalist,

Bristol (or Manchester or Birmingham or wherever) is just a point on the map at which things happen. If they happen in London, the district is usually mentioned, Ealing, or Chelsea, or Dulwich.'

Mr Roberts is right. I accept the rebuke on behalf of colleagues. Other newspapers, please copy.

24 APRIL 1983

Mr Nigel Jee, of Guernsey, writes: 'In the Channel Islands one of the shibboleths which distinguish an islander from a newcomer is that islanders live *in* Jersey or Guernsey or even Sark, outsiders think they live *on* these islands.' I asked a friend from the Isle of Wight whether her family lived in or on it. 'On', she said. The island's Director of Cultural Services, Mr Len Mitchell disagreed. 'It's in', he said firmly. (I knew the islanders were known as Vectians, from the Latin name for the island. The more colloquial word, Mr Mitchell says, is 'caulkhead', but only for those born there. Immigrants from the mainland, like himself, are called 'overners': from over the water.)

What about Skye, 535 square miles in area, bigger than the Isle of Wight, many, many times bigger than Guernsey? 'We live on the island', said a lady in the capital, Portree.

10 JULY 1983

The massive *Grammar of Contemporary English*, by Randolph Quirk and others, says: ' "In" is used for continents, countries, provinces and sizeable territories of any kind; but for towns, villages etc., either "at" or "in" is appropriate . . . A very large city, such as New York, London, or Tokyo, is generally treated as an area: "He works in London . . ." But one would treat it as a point on the map: "Our plane refuelled at London on its way from New York".' In a note it adds that 'the implications of "at", "on", and "in" are felt to be different' in ' "at the seaside (cf "on the coast"); "in the world" (cf "on (the) earth").' It goes on, ' "At the seaside" suggests a point of contact with the sea, rather than a one-dimensional coastline. "On the earth" sees the world as a surface (e.g. as a geologist might see it) rather than a place where people live.'

All very useful and authoritative, but difficulties remain. Shirley Wise, a schoolteacher, of Otley, near Leeds, is of the opinion that while 'it is certainly connected with size, it is also

49

to do with permanence: after a time people say they live *in* a place, even if it's a small village. We *always* say *in* Leeds. But my 12- to 14-year-olds often say *at* Leeds. One farmer's daughter confidently started an essay, "At France . . ." and a local woman asked me when discussing holidays, "Is it nice at Greece?" The children frequently say *at* London.'

Dr John Pettit, a consultant dermatologist in Kuala Lumpur, in Malaysia, writes: 'I have just prescribed two creams to a patient, one to be used *at* night and the other *in* the daytime. I also ask patients to come back *at* 9 a.m. *on* 17 May, and never use "at" for a date or "on" for a time. Can you tell me why?'

No. I can only, yet again, quote Dr Johnson on the capriciousness of usage (see TROTSKYIST/ITE).

IN/ON (liturgically speaking). After in/on islands (see IN/AT), Mr H. J. Corrie, of Maidenhead, asks why, in the Lord's Prayer, the minister in his church says 'Thy will be done, *on* earth as it is in heaven', whereas the Prayer Book says '*in* earth etc'.

This particular tussle has been going on for centuries. The original Greek has '. . . *hos en ourano kai epi ges*', 'as in heaven and [or so] on earth'. Then came the Vulgate (begun by St Jerome in 382) with '. . . *sicut in caelo et in terra*'. Note that the Latin *in* can also mean on. The Rev. Dr Gordon Huelin, lecturer in liturgy at King's College, London, knows of a thirteenth-century manuscript with 'Thy will also is in heaven so be on earth', but on the whole 'in' ruled the roost until about a hundred years ago, thanks largely to the Authorised Version (1611), the property of all believers of whatever denomination; Anglicans, of course, followed the Book of Common Prayer, produced in 1549 by Thomas Cranmer, for me the greatest master of prose in the language, not excepting the translators of the Authorised Version. Dr Huelin and the Methodist Rev. John Stacey agree that the change probably began some time after 1881, the year the Revised Version of the New Testament came out with 'Thy will be done, as in heaven, so *on* earth.'

'On' is now 'official'. It appeared in the experimental Anglican Alternative Services, Series Two, in 1967, and in the Methodist Service Book (which reflects Free Church usage generally) and the Roman Missal in 1975. But of course there is no 'official' version of this greatest of prayers. Even Matthew and Luke differ. In the Revised Standard Version and other recent translations the petition 'Thy will be done' does not appear in Luke at all.

25 SEPTEMBER 1983

KANGAROO COURT. In Vol. II of A Supplement to the OED you find: 'US, an improperly constituted court having no legal standing, e.g. one held by strikers, mutineers, prisoners etc.' But how, a colleague asks, did the term originate? The two-volume Webster's Third International gives no clue. Nor does the OED, whose examples go back to 1853: 'By a unanimous vote, Judge G – – – – –, was elected to the bench and the "Mestang" [variant of mustang] or "Kangaroo Court" was regularly organised' – from 'Stray Yankee in Texas.'

I consulted Australia House. Miss Athalie Colquhoun, head of the High Commission's Reference Library, promptly produced the following explanation (from *Australian Folk-lore: a Dictionary of Lore, Legends and Popular Allusions*, compiled by W. Fearn-Wannand, published by Lansdowne Press, Melbourne): 'Australians who went to the Californian gold-diggings in 1849 were called "Sydney Coves" . . . Because some of these men were ex-convicts, and most were rugged personalities without too much respect for law and order, they acquired an unsavoury reputation . . . and "Vigilante Committees", the first in United States history, were organised largely to deal with Australians' misdemeanours. From this meting out of "wild justice" to the Australians came the term "Kangaroo Court", an Americanism for the illegal trial of an Australian gold-digger.

'When in their turn American prospectors came to Australia with the gold rushes of the early 1850s they were treated with much hostility' because, an Australian has written, 'old colonialists resented the treatment of the "Sydney Ducks" in California . . .'

23 JANUARY 1983

K RASIS: '. . . the optimum mixture, balance or syntony of the major forces or processes of the body' — from *Celestial Lancets*, the elegantly entitled history of acupuncture by Lu Gwei-Djen and Joseph Needham (Cambridge University Press). 'Crasis', says the OED, derived from the Greek *krasis* and pronounced *craysis*, is 'the blending or combination of elements in the animal body, in herbs etc . . . Composition, constitution . . . *Obs.* [entry prepared for publication in 1893] . . . The combination of "humours" . . . constituting health or disease . . . ?*Obs.*' There is also a technical sense in Greek grammar which need not concern us here.

Interesting enough, and not contradictory of the Lu–Needham use of the word. But it is flat, neutral — '. . . a state of health or disease'; it quite lacks their clear conviction that *krasis* is a thoroughly good thing. How had they arrived at their definition? Dr (of science) Needham says he was brought up in a medical family: 'My father was a doctor [of medicine], and he used it in that sense.'

In Liddell and Scott *krasis* is defined as 'a mixing . . . of things which form a compound, as wine and water' — the ancient Greeks always diluted their wine, whence the demotic word for wine, *krasí*. Another sense is 'temperature of the air; temperate climate', and here a note of approval is apparent. It is confirmed in an 1875 abridgement of the lexicon, which has a reference to the Latin *temperies*: a *due* (my italics) mingling, mixture or tempering. What Drs Lu and Needham have done is to bring out this approbatory note, extending the sense of the word and enriching it. (See SYNTONY.)

11 DECEMBER 1983

Walton-on-Thames

DEAR MR SILVERLIGHT, *My copy of Bayley's dictionary (seventh edition, dated 1735) gives three definitions of 'crasis': (i) a mixture (ii) the use in grammar (iii) 'in Phyfic a proper Condition, Mixture, or Temperature of Humours in an Animal Body, fuch as conftitutes a State of Health.'*

Yours sincerely

A. W. (BILL) FULLER

LADY/WOMAN. It used to be so easy: I remember hearing as a child that a lady was someone who never used the word 'lady' – the correct word was 'woman'. Then doubts began to creep in. 'Don't touch the lady's dress', I would tell my own children if they tried to paw some unfortunate fellow bus-passenger. Nowadays one hears people talking about the 'tea-lady', or the 'launderette-lady'.

Of various dictionaries, the Longman Dictionary of Contemporary English (which is aimed at foreign students of English rather than native English speakers) has it about right: '. . . Lady is a polite but rather old-fashioned way of speaking about a woman. One may wish to use it (a) in her presence: "Please bring this lady a glass of beer", (b) with the old: it is pleasanter to call someone an old lady than an old woman . . .'

26 APRIL 1981

LAID BACK in Santa Barbara' – *Observer* Magazine cover story, 27 June. Readers asked about 'laid back'. I first became aware of the expression in October 1978, in an *Encounter* article by the novelist David Lodge, Professor of Modern English at Birmingham University. Headlined 'Where it's at: the poetry of psychobabble', the article was about life in Marin County, California, as told in a remarkable novel entitled *The Serial* by Cyra McFadden (Picador). In the last chapter, Professor Lodge wrote, the Holroyds (the couple whose marital 'scene' is 'the core of the plot') renew 'their marriage vows at a totally laid-back party where the Reverend Spike Thurston of the Radical Unitarian Church pronounces them conjoined persons and the guests shower them with brown rice'.

'Laid back', Professor Lodge says, dates from the 1930s. According to *Black Slang: A Dictionary of Afro-American Talk* (Routledge and Kegan Paul) it is jazz idiom for lagging behind the main rhythm, 'to go slow, unhassled'. In general domestic use it means very relaxed.

25 JULY 1982

LEVANTINE. A report in the *Spectator* on the Church of
England Synod last February contained the phrase 'a
lugubrious clergyman of levantine appearance'. The Levant,
from the French *lever* to rise, originally meant the East: where
the sun rises. Then the sense narrowed to those countries on
the shores of the eastern Mediterranean. Nowadays the word
has romantic if archaic associations (although the *Economist*
boasts a Levant Correspondent): 'Late in the evening of May
17, 1751, a boat carrying two British travellers anchored at a
small port in the Levant' – the opening sentence of Richard
Jenkyns's *The Victorians and Ancient Greece* (Blackwell); the small
port was the Piraeus.

Similarly 'levantine' used to be purely neutral in sense: of the
Levant. Not now. Whatever image the *Spectator* writer was
trying to evoke, it was not a favourable one: 'levantine', often
accompanied by 'oily', is invariably derogatory (which prompts
the perhaps irreverent thought, What kind of appearance did
that well-known Levantine Jesus have?).

The OED's first example with the derogatory sense is, 'I
must say that his [Bourbaki's] manner was very Levantine'
(*Daily News*, 23 September 1897). There is the pejorative verb
'levant', but that has a quite different derivation, from the
Spanish *levantar*, to lift: '*levantar la casa*, to break up house-
keeping, *levantar el campo*, to break up the camp' (OED).

3 APRIL 1983

LIKE/SUCH AS. 'Is there a real difference between them?'
a reader asks, quoting Dr Richard Hoggart's recent article in
The Observer, 'The Divisive Society', in which he wrote of the
'slow nature of change . . . in societies such as this'. I have
never been clear about the distinction – sometimes I felt one
was right, sometimes the other. Kingsley Amis, for instance,
could not have entitled his novel *Take a Girl Such As You*.
Dictionaries are not over-helpful, merely indicating that when
used to introduce examples the two can be interchangeable.
The OED article on 'like', prepared for publication in 1903,
provides one clue. 'In modern use', it says, 'like' often = 'such
as', quoting Robert Louis Stevenson in a letter, 'A critic like
you' (1899). This suggests, as I had thought, that 'like' is more
colloquial.

Lesley Burnett, who is revising the two-volume Shorter Oxford, agrees about the colloquial quality of 'like' – 'people tend to avoid it in written English', she says. But there is a semantic distinction too. 'Besides its informality, "like," when introducing examples, has an element of comparison. In the title "Take a Girl Like You," "You" could be an example, but it could also be someone similar. "Such as" has no such ambiguity.'

So 'such as' is more precise or, if you like, more prissy. The tone of the letter suggests that the reader who raised the matter with us thinks it is the latter.

9 MAY 1982

·OO. [Etym. obscure.] A privy, a lavatory' – Volume II of A Supplement to the Oxford English Dictionary. Ten years ago the historian Sir Steven Runciman wrote to Lord Lichfield, the photographer, that the story of the word's origin 'was told me by the Duke of Buccleuch's aunt, Lady Constance Cairns. Your relations feature largely in it. In 1867 (Lady Constance was not absolutely certain of the date) when the first Duke of Abercorn was Viceroy of Ireland there was a large houseparty at the Viceregal Lodge, and among the guests there was the Lord Lieutenant of County Roscommon, Mr Edward King Tennison, and his wife Lady Louisa, daughter of the Earl of Lichfield.

'Lady Louisa was, it seems, not very lovable; and the two youngest Abercorn sons, Lord Frederick and Lord Ernest, took her namecard from her bedroom door and placed it on the door of the only w.c. in the guest wing. So in those select ducal circles every one talked of going to Lady Louisa. Then people became more familiar – Jimmy Abercorn [the present duke] told me that when he was a boy one went to "Lady Lou" (though he had never been told who her ladyship was). Now in these democratic days the courtesy title has been dropped, and within the last 30 years or so – only really since the war – the term has seeped down into middle-class and even working-class usage. But it all really originated with your Hamilton uncles being ungallant to your Anson aunt; who I think should have her immortality recognised.'

The letter is quoted in Frank Muir's *A Book at Bathtime* (Heinemann).

12 JUNE 1983

55

'Loo' prompted more letters than any other word in the column's history. Most people said its source was the old Edinburgh cry 'Gardyloo' (apparently, says the Shorter Oxford, from *gare de l'eau*, 'pseudo-French' for *gare l'eau*, mind the water) before chamber-pots were emptied from tenement windows into the street. Andrée Bur-Brown, of Shenfield, in Essex, wrote, 'At the time of the French Revolution the term *lieux d'aisances* was very much in use (see La Petit Robert quoting Flaubert, "*Les lieux! Oui, ces braves latrines*").' The trouble with both these derivations is, as Frank Muir says in his *A Book at Bathtime*, that 'loo' seems to date back only to the late nineteenth century.

Mr Alan Smith, of Leighton Buzzard, wrote, 'Surely "loo" derives from the French *lieu*. Old Paris hotel lavatories have a notice "*On est prié de laisser ce LIEU aussi propre qu'on le trouve*".' (In Germany they have the same word, *der Locus*.) Still others derive it from 'Waterloo' — the first example in Volume II of A Supplement to the OED is James Joyce's 'O yes, *mon loup*. Waterloo. Watercloset', from *Ulysses* (1922). But it also describes as 'inconclusive' the examinations of possible sources by the late Professor Ross (of U and non-U fame), who 'favours derivation in some manner that cannot be demonstrated, from "Waterloo" '.

Vernon Noble, author of *Speak Softly: Euphemisms and Such*, suggests that 'it may have a nautical origin, from "looward" or "leeward" ' (from the Anglo-Saxon word for shelter). And A. Henry Bailey, of Portsmouth, says shepherds used 'lee', pronounced *lew*, for a shelter of hurdles which, 'when it was very windy', could be used 'to relieve nature'.

17 JULY 1983

LOST CAUSES.

Two or three years ago I was editing an article in which the phrase 'reached a crescendo' occurred. Irritably I substituted 'climax' only to learn that the use of 'climax' (which in Greek means ladder) in that sense was 'due to popular ignorance of the learned word' (OED). 'Properly' it meant 'an ascending ladder or scale'. Both the lexicographer (the great James Murray himself) and I, a century later, were fighting for lost causes: most dictionaries now accept 'crescendo' in the sense of peak.

I was reminded of all this by Kingsley Amis's review of The

Oxford Guide to English Usage in *The Observer* of 19 February. Apropos 'jejune', from the Latin *jejunus*, fasting, he wrote that its 'slide' in meaning from 'to do with fasting, scanty' to 'puerile' (third definition in the Concise Oxford) was started by 'the sort of journalist who is always on the look-out for classy new words but is too lazy to find out . . . where they come from'. In our files is a letter from Mr John Carthew, pupil of F. R. Leavis at Cambridge and now a lecturer in English literature at Tees-side Polytechnic. 'The "incorrect" use of "jejune" to mean naïve, crass, unsophisticated', he writes, 'seems to fill a long-felt need.' Certainly it *sounds* right, which, I suggest, rather than Mr Amis's suppositional journalist, explains the 'slide' in sense. Something similar is happening with 'effete'. Derived from the Latin for 'worn out by childbearing', 'properly' it means exhausted; increasingly it is used to mean effeminate.

My own pet regret is 'shrapnel'. 'Properly' it means a hollow projectile filled with lead pellets, invented by Lieut. Henry Shrapnel RA in the 1780s, timed to explode just short of its objective. That sense was already a lost cause in 1939 when I was a young artillery officer. In 1940 example in the forthcoming Volume IV of A Supplement to the OED has it meaning shell fragments. Winston Churchill denounced that sense as 'most erroneous', but it is now universal. And it still grates on me.

18 MARCH 1984

LOUNGE. In a letter to the Editor of *The Observer* the Rev. Paul Kelly, of Uxbridge, in Middlesex, writes apropos PARLOUR: 'We were not "grand". We were brought up in a large Victorian rectory in Devon and we always called our main sitting-room "the drawing room" and I shall continue to use that term to my dying day! I don't mind "parlour" − it has a pleasant, rather old-fashioned ring about it. The word that is right out as far as I am concerned is the horrible "lounge", which I'm glad John Silverlight didn't mention − it should only be used for hotels and airports.'

Mr Kelly is not alone in his sentiments. Except perhaps for 'toilet', no other word in the U/non-U business arouses more scorn than 'lounge' as a description of one's principal living room. I cannot see why − a lounge is where, presumably, one

57

lounges, i.e. reclines or relaxes, which is what I do in my sitting room. But the OED shows that as a verb, 'lounge' has a history of derogatory use going back at least to the 1500s. In 1879 the historian J. A. Froude wrote of someone who 'returned to Rome to lounge away his life in voluptuous magnificence'. 'Lounge lizard' was a put-down of the 1930s. ('Lounge' may have derived from the obsolete word 'lungis', from Longinus, 'apocryphal word of the centurion who pierced our Lord with a spear'. Again the usage is derogatory: 'lungis' means lout.)

'Lounge suit' has nothing derogatory about it — just the reverse. A colleague was due to accompany the Foreign Secretary on a tour of the Far East. Since he normally wears an anorak, jeans and open-necked shirt, he prudently checked on dress with the Foreign Office. 'Quite informal', he was told, 'just two or three lounge suits.' The Lord Chamberlain's office says invitations to royal garden parties at Buckingham Palace or Holyrood House carry the instruction, 'Morning Dress, Uniform or Lounge Suits'.

2 MAY 1982

LUDDITES: 'English artisans (1811—16) who raised riots for destruction of machinery' — Concise Oxford. The word has lost none of its resonance since those days, just the reverse. Sir Keith Joseph had only to say 'In some parts of the country there is Luddism' to get his message across to the Conservative Party Conference last October. Scars go deep on the other side too. Whatever the long-term benefits of the Industrial Revolution, in the short term it bore hard on working-class people. The period 1811—16 was one of depression, exacerbated by more than 20 years of war with the French. There was an appalling succession of bad harvests. Many families were getting 7 to 9 shillings a week; at one point in 1912 a 4 lb loaf of bread cost 1s. 8d. Workers had no representation. The government was fighting a powerful enemy abroad and went in fear of threats at home — there was a rising in Ireland in 1798, supported by a French landing. In 1799 the Combination Acts were passed, outlawing trade unions.

No section of society can have been worse off than textile workers, and their resentment of the new machines is understandable. For years the industry, vastly overgrown, had been sinking into chaos. Now the machines were further reducing the already falling number of jobs — and, so the workers claimed, were responsible for the production of garments inferior to those made 'in a tradesmanlike manner'. Machine-breaking erupted in 1811 among the 'stockingers' (hosiery framework knitters) and laceworkers centred on Nottingham. It spread to the Lancashire cotton weavers, then to the West Riding 'croppers', who finished woollen cloth by raising its nap and 'cropping' it with 4ft-long shears. Armed masked men invaded villages by night smashing the machines. Messages left behind demanding concessions were often signed 'General (or Captain) Ludd'.

The origin of the name 'Ludd' is obscure. According to one source it was 'said to derive from a youth named Ludlam, a reckless character, who, when his father, a framework knitter, told him one day to "square his needles", squared them effectively by taking up his hammer and beating them into a heap' (*The Risings of the Luddites*, published by Frank Cass).

All told the Luddites, including their families, probably never numbered as many as 10 000, but 12 000 troops were called out against them (four years earlier Wellington, then Sir Arthur Wellesley, sailed for Portugal with 9000 men to take on Napoleon's marshals). By mid-1812 the movement had been practically stamped out; 40 men were hanged, 36 transported, 13 jailed. There was another brief outbreak in 1816–17, followed by more hangings, transportations and jailings.

It was all very reprehensible, no doubt; useless, too. Technological change is as irresistible as change in the use of language. But it is worthwhile recalling conditions at a time when there were no state benefits to cushion unemployment and so understanding, at least partly, why those out-of-work stockingers, croppers and weavers, watching their families starve to death, turned to violence. To them and their like, as E. P. Thompson writes in his magisterial *Making of the English Working Class*, the rewards of 'the march of progress' always seemed to be gathered by someone else.

16 DECEMBER 1979

MISSILE/MISSAL. A reader is distressed by the American pronunciation of the word for 'a deadly weapon of war' as if it were that different thing, 'an old, beautifully illuminated manuscript or book'. I must report that her forebears would find nothing wrong with American usage; they would with ours. My authority is Professor A. C. Gimson, editor of Everyman's English Pronouncing Dictionary, who, in turn, quotes dictionaries by Thomas Sheridan (1780) and Robert Walker (1825) to show that many '-ile' words besides missile − agile, nubile, reptile, volatile, etc. − used to rhyme with pencil. So did subtile (subtle), despite the spelling. They also show exile, gentile, infantile and senile rhyming with file. That is modern American usage too.

Thomas Sheridan, according to the Dictionary of National Biography, father of Richard Brinsley and son of Thomas, 'schoolmaster and friend of Swift', was an actor and 'orthoepist' ('one who treats of the prununication of words' − OED). In 1796 a Mr S. Jones brought out a book, *Sheridan Improved*, in which 'the discordances of that celebrated orthoepist were avoided and his improprieties corrected'.

7 FEBRUARY 1982

MISTLETOE MYSTERIES.

What with the kissing and giggling and general jollity associated with mistletoe, it comes as a slight shock to find Shakespeare writing of 'Trees . . . Orecome with . . . baleful Misselto' (*Titus Andronicus* II iii 95). The mistletoe was certainly full of bale for the Norse god of light, Baldur the Beautiful. After he had dreamt that his life was in danger his mother, Frigga, called on all living things to swear not to harm him. However, she neglected to put the oath to the mistletoe, and it was a branch of mistletoe, flung by his blind brother Hoder, that killed him. There was also the Elizabethan dramatist Robert Greene, who wrote, 'None comes neere the fume of the Misselden but he waxeth blind' (1590).

Mostly, however, mistletoe is the great healer − one of its names is All Heal. One OED example, dated 1550, reads, 'Mysceltowe layd to the head draweth out the corrupt humores.' Again, 'The mistletoe of the oak had such repute for "helping" diseases incidental to infirmity and old age, that it was called *Lignum Sanctae Crucis*, Wood of the Holy Cross' (1866). But according to the Encyclopaedia Britannica, *Viscum Album*, the 'traditional mistletoe of literature and Christmas celebrations', is 'most abundant on apple trees, poplars, linden and hawthorns. It is rarely found on oaks.'

Mistletoe is the Golden Bough of antiquity, whence the title of Sir James Frazer's book. In Welsh it has the name 'tree of pure gold', according to *Christmas in Ritual and Tradition*, by Clement A. Miles, who quotes Frazer as writing that 'the sun's golden fire was believed to be emanation from the mistletoe, in which the life of the oak, whence fire was kindled, was held to reside.'

19 DECEMBER 1982

MR, MRS, MISS, MS. I have never liked being addressed

as 'Dear John Silverlight'. People not on Christian name terms with me, I felt, should address me as 'Mr'. On the other hand, for some time, when addressing envelopes, I have tended not to use the first three titles quoted here, 'Ms' I rejected out of hand and 'Esq' I dropped years ago except when writing to accountants or lawyers, and not always to them.

Now if this feature has any guiding theme, beyond the expression of a fascination with words, it is belief in the uselessness of fighting usage, although I shall continue to deprecate some of its effects, e.g. the confusion of 'refute' and 'deny', or, for that matter, between 'deprecate' and 'depreciate'. (What I am *not*, to the disappointment of some colleagues, is a self-appointed 'guardian of the purity of the language'.)

So, in earnest of that belief, 'Dear JS' it is. That declaration brings with it an unlooked-for bonus. If a woman correspondent did not make it apparent whether or not she was married, I was always nervous of offending a 'Mrs' by calling her 'Miss' and vice versa. Now I shan't have to use either of them — or 'Ms'.

29 MARCH 1981

London SW5

DEAR MR SILVERLIGHT, *I am always annoyed at having to sign myself 'Miss D.B.' instead of 'D.B.' as I can do when I write using German or French. Automatically I am addressed in replies as* Frau *or* Madame, *as I am always when I speak to people in those countries (or Italy — Signore) in shops or wherever. I wish 'Mrs' were adopted here at least for older women. 'Ms' I think bloody awful.*

Yours sincerely

DORIS BAUM

N̄AFF.

A reader, Miss Yolande Yates, has done considerable research on what the *Daily Express* (17 September) has described as the 'newest four-letter word'. Its adjectival sense is apparent from one of Miss Yates's references: 'The British don't like something as naff as this [foil-covered, triangular- or oblong-shaped wine containers]' – Jill Goolen, wine expert of BBC2's 'Food and Drink', 28 July. Nor is there any doubt about the sense of the word in its other use, 'Naff off!'

Paul Beale, who is revising the late Eric Partridge's *Dictionary of Slang*, has traced the expression in its sense of 'tatty' to theatrical *lingua franca* in the 1950s. As for 'naff off', long before Princess Anne was quoted as saying it, Ronnie Barker had made it famous in the BBC television series 'Porridge', first shown in 1974. Dick Clement, who, with Ian La Frenais, wrote the script, says they were looking for an expletive with bite that would not be offensive. Then they remembered adapting Keith Waterhouse's novel *Billy Liar* (first published 1959) for the stage. There it was, page 37, 'Naff off!'

And where did Keith Waterhouse get it? From his RAF service: 'naffing' was a substitute for the usual age-old obscenity. Here, perhaps, is where the two senses meet. The NAAFI (Navy, Army and Air Force Institutes) provides canteens and shopping facilities for the Forces. Could it, Paul Beale wonders, have been the 'naffness' of the NAAFI that prompted the expression?

24 OCTOBER 1982

N̄AVVY,

from 'navigator': 'A labourer employed in excavating etc. for canals, railways, roads etc.' – Concise Oxford. In the early 1970s a nephew of mine, then aged 22, worked on the Exeter–Plymouth stretch of the A38. What did he call himself? 'A labourer.' Not a navvy? 'No.' Then he thought again. 'The older men', he said, 'called themselves navvies.' The

Federation of Civil Engineering Contractors confirms my impression that the word is obsolete professionally: instead the Federation's Working Rule Agreement now refers to General Civil Engineering Operatives. Anthony Trollope would not have approved. In *The Three Clerks*, which appeared in 1853 when 'navvy' was a comparatively recent coinage (the first OED example is dated 1832), he created the imaginary Civil Service Department of Internal Navigation, 'not unusually denominated "the Infernal Navigation" . . . The navvies of Somerset House are known all over London.'

All this is only an excuse to mention Trollope, who died a hundred years ago last Monday. The Trollope boom is gratifying. However, to addicts it seems that his stature is still not appreciated. There is the idea, for instance, that he shies away from sexuality. One academic (certainly not hostile) writes, 'Trollope's heroines are of their time in being sexless', and Lily Dale, of *The Small House at Allington*, is instanced (Laurence Lerner, in his introduction to the Penguin *The Last Chronicle of Barset*). It is Lily Dale, explaining why she still loves the man who jilted her, who says, 'When he kissed me I kissed him again and I longed for his caresses. I seemed to live only that he might caress me.'

If that is sexless, I do not know what sex is.

12 DECEMBER 1982

NEWBOLT'S poem beginning 'There's a breathless hush in the close tonight' was the first I ever learnt by heart. Seeing it echoed in an *Observer* story 'The skeleton in Winchester's cricket cupboard' (24 April) sent me back to it.

It deals with a cricket match ('An hour to play and the last man in'), then a desert action ('The Gatling's jammed and the Colonel dead'). The last stanza describes how the Old School's sons all bear 'the word' ('Play up! play up! and play the game') through life and, falling, fling it 'to the host behind'.

I was puzzled by the title, 'Vitaï Lampada'. It looked like 'lamp of life' (which it is, roughly), but what had that to do with cricket and Gatling guns? The clue is in that third stanza, which echoes a passage in the Roman poet Lucretius: '. . . Some nations wax and others wane and in a short space of time the generations of living things change and, like runners, hand on the torch of life.' The torch is tradition, and the metaphor is from the Greek relay race in which a burning torch was passed from hand to hand. (*Vitaï*, incidentally, is an old genitive singular of *vita*.)

The poem's date is interesting too, 1892. Henry Newbolt was a poet of the twilight of Empire – Kipling was a near contemporary; so was A. E. Housman – and his verse, for all its robustness, has a note of *angst* about it. The desert action of the second stanza, with its 'square that broke', suggests the Sudan. The death of Gordon, in 1885, was still unavenged. The Boer War was only seven years away.

8 MAY 1983

The Percival Library, Clifton College, Bristol

DEAR MR SILVERLIGHT, *You must, I think, be right when you suggest the Sudan for the setting of the second stanza. Newbolt doesn't seem to have had in mind a specific historical event, but a brass in chapel lists the five Old Cliftonians who died in that campaign.*

The cricket match itself was a junior house match. Newbolt himself was 'the last man in', and the Captain who proffered the exemplary advice, Charles Chetwode Hardy, died in 1966 at the ripe old age of 101.

Yours sincerely

DAVID REED, *Librarian*

Cullercote, North Shields

DEAR SIR, *I recall hearing an account of a talk given at a Military Historical Society meeting in 1966. From it I inferred that the battle referred to in the poem was Abu Klea, when Kipling's Fuzzy Wuzzy – 'you big black boundin' beggar' – broke the square of the First Bn. the Royal Sussex Regiment. I was therefore surprised to read recently in Christopher Wood's 'Victorian Panorama: Paintings of Victorian Life' (Faber and Faber, 1976) that Newbolt was discussing Isandhlwana. The author writes (p. 243), 'Fripps's picture of the last heroic defenders gives substance both to the lines and spirit of* **Vitai Lampada.'** *However, I incline to the view that the battle took place in the Sudan. I am not very knowledgeable about the terrain*

in Zululand, but the proximity of the Tugela River to Isandhlwana
does not suggest desert conditions.

Yours faithfully,
W. A. MILLER

Mr Miller's reference to Isandhlwana interests me. In the first draft of the article I wrote, '. . . The desert action could have been suggested by Isandhlwana where, three years earlier, a British force had been wiped out by Zulus.' Then I remembered that Isandhlwana was fought in 1879, not 1889, and decided that the longer lapse of time made that battle less likely to have been in Newbolt's mind. That, together with the poem's specific reference to 'desert' made me plump for the Sudan. Mr Wood does not disagree. In his book, he says, he was merely emphasising the similarity in spirit between the painting and the poem.

NOMENCLATOR. A footnote in Peter Medawar's highly
rewarding collection of essays, *Pluto's Republic*, refers to William Whewell, 'polymath and nomenclator'.

Nomenclator, it was clear from context, means someone who names things. (In ancient Rome it meant the slave whose duty it was to name the people his master met 'during a political campaign' − Webster's Collegiate.) Whewell (1794−1866) was a joiner's son who became Master of Trinity College, Cambridge. His first degree was in mathematics (Second Wrangler); he was ordained priest in 1825; in 1828 he was appointed Professor of Mineralogy; in 1837 he was made President of the Geological Society; he became Professor of Moral Philosophy in 1838; a polymath indeed. In 1840 he invented the words 'scientist' ('We need very much a name to describe a cultivator of science in general. I should incline to call him a Scientist' − OED) and 'physicist'. Other words he invented or helped to invent include (with Michael Faraday) 'anode' and 'cathode', the names for the poles of an electrolytic cell, as well as 'anion', 'cation' and 'ion' (electrically-charged particles), and (with the geologist Charles Lyell) 'Eocene', 'Miocene' and 'Pliocene'.

Sir Peter has told me of a correspondence in which 'Faraday had suggested "zincode" and "platinode", "eastode" and "westode", "volteode" and "galvanode". Whewell must have got fed up with all this because the correspondence ends with Whewell's "My dear Sir . . . I am disposed to recommend anode and cathode" – and so they have remained ever since.'

The book's Introduction explains the title: 'A good many years ago a neighbour whose sex chivalry forbids me to disclose, exclaimed on hearing of my interest in philosophy, "Don't you just adore Pluto's Republic?" ' Citizens of this intellectual underworld include Teilhard de Chardin and Arthur Koestler, but the most prominent are 'IQ psychologists and psychotherapists who apply psychotherapy to the victims of organic diseases of the body'.

11 MARCH 1984

NOT TO MENTION. Mr Jo Grimond recently wrote,

apropos the Franks Report on the Falklands crisis: 'Over the past 50 years, while many individual foreign officers have been percipient and right, the Foreign Office itself has been blind and wrong on many major issues, e.g. appeasement, the Middle East . . . not to mention its curious inability to recognise its own traitors' (*Spectator*, 29 January).

My first, perverse reaction was, Why mention it then? Then I thought of the many similar expressions: not to speak of; to say nothing of; it goes without saying; needless to say – after all of which one goes on to say precisely what one has just said does not need saying. At least that is what it looks like, superficially. The literary device meiosis (from the Greek for diminution) is used to understate in order to emphasise; an example in Fowler is 'He didn't half swear' for 'He swore horribly.' 'Not to mention' etc. serve the same purpose.

Many (most?) languages have equivalents: *pour ne pas nommer, ça va sans dire, sans parler de* (French); *yia na mi poume* – 'in order that we should not say' (Greek); *ne emlitsuk* – 'not to mention' (Hungarian); *nie mówiac już o* – 'not speaking already about' (Polish); and the German *ganz zu schweigen* – 'totally to keep silent'. The full title of Jerome K. Jerome's book is *Three Men in a Boat To Say Nothing of the Dog!* In German: *'Drei Mann in einem Boot. Ganz zu Schweigen vom Hund!*

6 MARCH 1983

LD BILL. Mr Arthur Moyse, of West Kensington, writes asking 'how the term "Old Bill" came to be given to the police. I have asked various policemen without success, and Eric Partridge, in his Dictionary of Slang, refers to Bruce Bairnsfather's Old Bill of the First World War, which I think must be wrong. My useless guess is that it is derived from the working-class song "Won't you come home, Bill Bailey," and the Old Bailey (Central Criminal Court).'

The eighth edition of Partridge, due to be published this year, edited by Paul Beale, has, as the fourth definition of the term, 'A policeman: cant and fringe-of-the-underworld slang; since 1950s, possibly earlier . . .' In a letter Paul Beale quotes from *The Signs of Crime: A Field Manual for Police* by David Powis, a senior Met. officer: 'Bill, or Old Bill. Specifically, the Metropolitan Police and, generally, all police . . . ' Mr Beale also writes: 'My own theory is that the term goes back possibly to the pre-World War Two police, many of whom would have been World War One veterans with walrus moustaches like Bairnsfather's Old Bill – Press photos of the General Strike, the Abdication, etc. bear this out. I think that Arthur Moyse's guess is far from "useless." It seems to me a very likely source.'

I first met the expression in Mr Moyse's letter. Now I come across it all the time. An Islington newspaper carried the headline 'Kids meet "Old Bill" ' over a story of a policeman presenting prizes at a school for handicapped children. And, of course, it keeps cropping up in the engaging Thames Television series 'Minder' – it occurred in last week's episode and I could not help feeling pleased that I, brought up in America, was able to explain it to my London-born wife.

26 FEBRUARY 1984

PARADIGM, an example or pattern, has been frowned on as a vogue word, unfairly. For one thing it has been around for a long time: the OED's first example is from Caxton's *The Golden Legend* (1483): 'We now have no interpreter of the parables or paradigms.' But a paradigm (it rhymes with time) is not just any example; it is one that is particularly clear. The specialised sense gives the full force: example of a word in all its forms – *amo, amas, amat*, etc., or, in English, man, man's, men, men's. I like the use I saw in the *Radio Times* recently when the producer of the BBC television series 'Private Schultz' said that in its theme – 'cold German logic wedded to grandiose madness' – he saw 'a paradigm of the Nazi psyche'.

To scientists a paradigm is the structure within which they perceive their knowledge. Every now and then revolutions occur as when, say, Copernicus rejected the Ptolemaic system of astronomy and sought his own paradigm, or when Newtonian physics began to break down and Einstein, Thompson and Planck came along. Indeed, to one eminent historian of science, Thomas Kuhn, scientific progress is the succession of such 'paradigm shifts'.

23 AUGUST 1981

Sir Peter Medawar, in his latest book, *Pluto's Republic* (1982), writes that Halley's prediction in 1704 that the comet now bearing his name would return in 1758 'made a tremendous impression and seemed to many people to be the very paradigm of all that was truly "scientific" '.

*P*ARADIGMS LOST: *Reflections on Literacy and Its Decline*

(Chatto and Windus) is by John Simon who, says the blurb, is 'renowned for his columns in *Esquire* and elsewhere'. Mr Simon is 'reasonably sure' he is not 'merely a *laudator temporis acti*' (yearner for the good old days). Perhaps, but he describes the loss of the second person singular pronoun 'thou' as conceivably the 'greatest of English losses *vis-à-vis* the other European languages'. Some of us agree with Professor Randolph Quirk (who, predictably, is not admired by Mr Simon) that the loss, which occurred some 300 or 400 years ago, was one of our greatest gains.

However, Mr Simon's heart is obviously in the right place, and will no doubt give much pleasure with his relentless citing of (mainly American) offences against the language. As for me, I agree with Horace in the poem just quoted that the years, as they pass, take away good things but bring good things too. I am also impenitently permissive – a grievous sin in Mr Simon's eyes – and was mildly irritated to be described in a letter to the Editor as someone who 'sets out to instruct us in the correct use of words'. I set out to inform and, if possible, to entertain: the prime duties of a journalist.

25 OCTOBER 1981

In commenting on John Simon's Paradigms Lost *John Silverlight declares himself 'impenitently permissive' in matters of language, and quotes Horace to the effect that the years (i.e. usage) bring good things as well as take them away: implying, I suppose, the common argument that English has always been changing and hence it is vain/improper/ ridiculous to object to any innovation/catachresis/deformity whatsoever. I wonder if he heard the talk* Words *(Radio 3, the same morning), in which John Wain remarked that change in the past was slow and measured whereas today, mainly because of TV, it is effected continuously and violently. What we have now is not so much linguistic development as a series of jolts — imposition rather than selection by the test of time. The difference might be compared to war by bow-and-arrow (which, obviously, the race has survived) and nuclear war (which could jolt us to pieces). Whatever is, is right?*

D. J. ENRIGHT

See PURISTS.

PARAMETER is another fashionable word I am nervous of.

However . . . I came across it when working on an article on euthanasia. One of the difficult questions in this most difficult issue is sometimes that of deciding when a person is dead. 'In grappling with such problems', the late Ian Ramsey, then Bishop of Durham, suggested, 'it is helpful to regard death as a multiparameter concept — a function of various factors', e.g. heart and brain activity.

Ramsey, before going into the Church, had been a mathematician, and would have known about parameters, the numbers that determine the shape of mathematical objects such as ellipses and parabolas. By extension the word has come to mean 'any distinguishing or defining characteristic . . .' (forthcoming Vol. III of A Supplement to the Oxford English Dictionary). Collins gives the example 'A designer must work within the parameters of budget and practicality.' E. P. Thompson, quoted in *The Observer*, has spoken about 'the break up of the parameters of the Cold War' (and was taken to task by Paul Johnson for using the word).

Certainly it is misused (although it can loosely mean

boundary, it does not mean perimeter, which is the length around something) but, for people who know what they are talking about, it has its uses.

13 SEPTEMBER 1981

Canon H. J. Hamerton, of Bramhope, Leeds, wrote: 'I had the highest regard for the late Bishop Ramsey, and I considered his premature death to be the greatest blow to the Church of England since the death of William Temple. But I never suspected that he was as precocious as John Silverlight indicated in his "Words" column last week, in which he said that Ramsey was a mathematician before going into the Church. Since Ian Ramsey went into the Church at his baptism, and since I am pretty certain it was an infant baptism, you can see how precocious John Silverlight has made him out to be.

'Anyone who sets out to instruct us in the correct use of words (and I value this column) should beware of the catachrestic use of "going into the Church" to describe Ordination.'

I replied accepting Canon Hamerton's rebuke for using the phrase 'going into the Church' instead of 'being ordained'. I added that I fully shared his regard for Bishop Ramsey and thanked him for his kind words about 'Words'. I did not accept his description of me as setting out 'to instruct us in the correct use of words' (see PARADIGMS LOST). When, while preparing this book for publication, I sought his permission to reproduce his letter, he replied that although he had not kept the correspondence he remembered 'feeling a little chastened by your kind letter and by some comment in a later column which made me feel I had expressed myself more strongly than I had intended'.

PARLOUR. Neighbours who are converting their house are renaming the sitting room the 'parlour'. I was faintly startled, having been brought up to think that one of the marks of the middle (or professional) classes was that we had sitting rooms, used all the time, whereas the lower (or working) classes had parlours, opened only for visitors. We never spoke of 'drawing room' – altogether too grand.

Parlour originally meant a room in a monastery for

conversation (it comes from the French *parler*) with people from outside or among inmates. Then it came to mean a smaller room in a mansion, dwelling house, town hall, etc. for private conversation, 'e.g. a banker's parlour, the Mayor's Parlour . . . Hence, in a private house, the ordinary sitting room' (OED). Chaucer, in 'Troilus and Criseyde' (1374), writes of 'a paved parlour'.

Mayors still have parlours, used mainly for entertaining; bamkers, alas, no longer do, not even in the older, smarter banks, except for the Bank of England, where The Parlours are offices for Governors and Directors. At one time, however, the Bank was in the Grocers' Hall, where the main business went on; next to it was the Great Parlour, for more private transactions. Incidentally, the Bank has a Drawing Office, once the Withdrawing Office, where funds are withdrawn. 'Drawing room' was once 'withdrawing room', to which ladies retired after dinner.

I like the revival of 'parlour' in SW13.

28 MARCH 1982

Blackrock, Co. Dublin

1 Samuel IX, 22 *(Authorised Version).*

Yours faithfully
NORAH DRAPER

('And Samuel took Saul and his servant, and brought them into the parlour, and make them sit in the chiefest place among them that were bidden, which were about thirty persons.')

PARSON'S NOSE. Why, a reader asks, is the rump of a
chicken (or turkey or goose or any other fowl) so called? Examples in the Oxford English Dictionary indicate that it was regarded as a titbit or, in Longfellow's phrase, an 'epicurean morsel' (1839) and therefore reserved for the parson. Another example describes it as a 'savoury mouthful. Sometimes called the Pope's nose.' Eric Partridge, in A Dictionary of Slang, traces 'Pope's nose' to the second edition of Francis Grose's A Classical Dictionary of the Vulgar Tongue (1788).

There is a similar, even older expression: 'Husband, pray cut me the Popes Eye [lymphatic gland surrounded with fat] out of the Leg of Mutton, I'le try if I can eat a bit of it' – OED example from John Wade's 'Vinegar and mustard; or wormwood lectures for every day in the week' (1673). The German for Pope's eye is *Pfaffensbisschen*, priest's bit, probably, says the OED, 'as being a titbit which the priest was supposed to claim; in French *oeil de Judas*'.

Tastes change and what was regarded as a delicacy then is not regarded as one now. As a child I disliked the parson's nose but put up with it if I could have a drumstick. My children used to put up with a drumstick if they could have breast too. The parson's nose they refused to look at.

20 DECEMBER 1981

P EJORATION. 'Permissiveness,' someone writes in *The Listener*, 'has produced its own orthodoxy and as such is fit to be ridiculed along with Mrs Thatcher, Prince Charles and the rest of them.' Mrs Thatcher has been quoted as speaking of the 'permissive claptrap' of the 1960s, which 'set the scene for a society in which the old virtues of discipline and self-restraint were denigrated'.

When my children were little I prided myself on being a permissive – not an indulgent – parent. My principle was to let them do what they wanted as long as it did not harm them or bother other people – including my wife and myself.

Already, however, the word was losing its neutral sense ('giving permission', Concise Oxford, 1964 edition). Volume III of A Supplement to the Oxford English Dictionary has this example, dated 1956: '. . . in the face of the permissive tendencies of the age there is not much respect for rules.' The Longman Dictionary of Contemporary English defines 'permissive' as 'allowing a great deal of, or too much, freedom, especially in sexual matters'. It is a classic example of 'pejoration' – 'semantic change whereby a word acquires unfavorable connotations' (Collins).

See AMELIORATION.

30 MAY 1982

PESSIMAL. Dr R. N. Hardy, Lecturer in Physiology at Cambridge University writes apropos of POLICE TALK: 'I am sure there are potentially valuable words as yet undiscovered by the English language. I append one such that occurred to me recently when writing a scientific paper in which I was discussing results obtained in a variety of experimental conditions. The word "optimal" came readily to hand in order to describe the most favourable combinations of conditions, but I discovered that there is no convenient antithesis to optimal. I therefore invented "pessimal" − but, alas, did not have the courage to use it − to describe the worst conceivable set of circumstances.

'I have spoken to some classics of my acquaintance who assure me that the Latin root (*pessimus* = worst) is perfectly respectable. So I wonder whether you would consider promoting its adoption.'

Useful neologisms survive, useless ones don't. I think Dr Hardy's is useful.

23 MAY 1982

Scarborough

Dr Hardy may be encouraged in his desire to promote the use of the word 'pessimal' to know of the following definition from Webster's Third New International Dictionary (1961): Pessimal: of, relating to, or constituting a pessimum; worst (a pessimal environment).

F. M. WEPSIEC

PLEASE. One of the Americanisms I was laughed out of when I came to this country as a small boy was 'you're welcome' in response to 'thank you'. There were others but now, some decades later, that is the only one I regret giving up. I do not care for the stock BrE (British English) responses: 'don't mention it' and 'not at all' I find ungracious; 'it's a pleasure' too often simply is not true.

The obvious word is 'please'. Germans have *bitte*, Italians *prego*, Russians *pozhaluysta* (which sounds like *pazhalsta*) and the Greeks have *parakaló*. In contrast the French, with *pas de quoi* and *de rien*, and Spanish (*de nada*) are closer to us. I like the

Finnish exchange: 'thank you' is *kiitos* and that is also the usual response. (I have heard 'thank you' in response to 'thank you' in this country too, but not so often.)

If, as some people gloomily prophesy, AmE (American English) does eventually take over — and I do not believe it will — I shall at least welcome 'you're welcome'.

15 NOVEMBER 1981

Rickmansworth

DEAR MR SILVERLIGHT, *I was surprised to read in your column that the expression 'You're welcome' is considered to be American. I have used it all my life.*

I was born in Devon in the late 1920s of Devonshire parents, from whom, presumably, I learnt it, and in my 50-odd years of saying 'You're welcome' frequently, only one person has commented on its use.

Yours sincerely

DOROTHY V. CROSS (MRS)

Kilnaleck

DEAR SIR, *'You're welcome' is by far the most common response to 'Thank you' here in Ireland. In England (West Country), where I lived for four years, while I was laughed out of some Irishisms, 'You're welcome', which I must have used almost daily, caused no remarks (to my face anyway!).*

Yours sincerely

PATRICK MCMANUS

Wrexham

DEAR JOHN SILVERLIGHT, *The response 'You're welcome' may sound strange to English ears. In Wales, however, it is a most common response to 'Thank you', albeit most often in our native tongue, i.e. 'Croeso'. (I write as an almost monoglot Welsh-speaking Welshman.)*

Apropos American/English differences I am reminded of the quotation (Churchill) to the effect that the Americans and English are the same people divided by a common language.

It occurs to me that the two peoples are divided most obviously by their asses/arses. One often hears in American films a tough sergeant

74

telling his troops to 'Get up off your asses', when presumably he means 'arses'. Equally the public school upper-crust Englishman will often refer to another as 'silly arse' when clearly he means a 'silly ass'. As one who is trying to make some sense out of English pronunciation I find this most confusing.

Yours in perplexity

ALUN DAVIES

Hartola, Finland

SIR, *Finns do say 'kiitos' after having given, rather than accepted, something. This corresponds to our British 'Thank you' to a customer as he leaves the shop, i.e. 'Thank you for your custom'. The usual response to 'kiitos' is 'ole hyvä', or, in formal situations, 'olkaa hyvää'. This is roughly the equivalent of the American 'You're welcome'. Strangely the Finnish has no word for 'please'!*

Yours faithfully

R. ROBINSON

P̄LURALS. Mr Michael McCrum, Master of Corpus Christi College, Cambridge, writes: 'Now that Greek and Latin are taught to so few, the future of English words formed from neuter plurals in those languages is bleak. "Agenda" as a singular has become almost wholly acclimatised, and even pedants and purists, too craven to say "agenda are . . .", take refuge in circumlocutions such as "agenda paper" to keep the word's plural flag flying.

'But perhaps "bacteria", "curricula" and "phenomena" can be saved. Is it not useful rather than pedantic to distinguish one "bacterium" from another? Likewise the proper use of "curricula" is probably guaranteed by its being restricted to educational contexts. The Infant Phenomenon too, thanks to the success of the staged version of "Nicholas Nickleby", will ensure that the word holds its own as a Greek singular for a few years more, and that people will continue to use "phenomena" as a plural.

'The greatest confusion is over "data" and "media". Reputable scientists do not hesitate to write such sentences as "the data is exceptional". As for "media", the word's fate to be singular is perhaps sealed. Do not the "media" appear to the public as a single amorphous amalgam (often of hostile influence) rather than individually identifiable as newspapers, magazines, radio and television?'

Mr McCrum, a classic (as classical scholars call themselves at Cambridge), may be right about 'media'. But (to quote the American columnist William Safire) 'we should resist the notion that "the media" is one vast, amorphous lump. By preserving the plural form we assert the diverse idea.'

26 JUNE 1983

POLICE TALK. One night last autumn there was a bomb
attack on the London home of Sir Michael Havers, the Attorney General. Early next morning, so two readers reported, Independent Radio News quoted the head of Scotland Yard's Anti-Terrorist Squad, Commander Mike Richards, as saying, 'We are containing the area, and forensication will begin at first light.' After a moment's hostile reaction I quite liked 'forensication', especially after looking up 'forensic' in Longman's Dictionary of Contemporary English: 'Relating to the tracking of criminals.'

Miss Valerie Adams, of University College, London, author of *An Introduction to Modern English Word Formation*, comments: ' "Forensication" strikes me as quite a useful innovation. I take it to be specific in meaning — something like "examination of the area for concrete evidence which may later be useful in legal proceedings".'

Any one word, however unattractive at first sight, that does the work of fifteen others has my backing too.

14 MARCH 1982

Manchester

DEAR SIR, *John Silverlight defends the word 'forensication' because it means 'examination of the area for concrete evidence which may later be used in legal proceedings', and one word is better than 15. I think it means 'looking for clues', and that four syllables are better than five.*

Yours faithfully

PETER EVERETT

DEAR SIR, Peter Everett's letter illustrates a common fault of those who seek to simplify English, namely insufficient attention to the meaning of the English they propose to simplify.

Mr Everett ignores Valerie Adams's 'concrete evidence' and 'useful in legal proceedings'. An archaeologist sifting a site for concrete evidence of, say, pre-Roman occupation, is not engaged in forensication since he has no intention of using the evidence in legal proceedings. So too a policeman making verbal inquiries may be looking for clues with no intention of presenting in court the fragmentary hints he gets since they are not concrete evidence of anything.

A compiler of crossword puzzles would, by Mr Everett's definition, be engaged in forensication.

Yours faithfully

J. KEITH R. BARNETT

PRESENTLY.

'. . . Sir Geoffrey Howe . . . ex-Law Officer, ex-Chancellor, presently Foreign Secretary' — John Cole, the BBC's Political Editor in his ever-excellent column in *The Listener* of 14 July. On the same day Mrs Sheila Dorrell, of Barnes, in south-west London, wrote to *The Observer* about the difference between the sense of 'presently' in England (soon) and in Scotland (at present; Mr Cole is an Ulsterman). The latter use, the OED says in its entry, prepared for publication in 1908, has been obsolete since the seventeenth century in literary English but is common 'in Scots writers', and British desk dictionaries agree that the primary sense of 'presently' in Scotland and the United States is 'at present'. In Scotland, perhaps; I am doubtful about the US. According to Webster's Dictionary of Synonyms, 'a little while' is the primary sense of 'presently'.

However, the John Cole quotation bears out the observation of Volume III of A Supplement to the OED that the sense of 'at present' is being revived. A pity. 'At present' and 'currently' are no longer than 'presently' and are less ambiguous. The best is 'now': as clear as any and shortest of all.

24 JULY 1983

Mr John Ayto, of Brighton, a lexicographer, observes that

'presently' is 'just one of a group of words that point up intriguingly how language change reflects human nature, in this case the tendency to procrastinate'. He cites 'directly' which, especially in American usage, has come to mean 'shortly' as well as 'immediately' − examples in Volume I of A Supplement to the OED includes: 'Supper'll be ready directly', *Moby Dick* (1851), and 'Scarlett . . . leaned over the bannisters. "I'll be down terrectly, Rhett," she called', *Gone with the Wind* (1936). However, Mr Ayto writes, 'I suspect "directly" still suggests less delay than "presently".

'Going further back, "anon" meant "at once" in Old and Middle English; in Shakespeare's time it meant "soon"; now it's decidedly non-committal − "I'll see you anon". But the most striking example is "soon", which in Old English times meant "straightaway"! Nowadays to get something in a hurry you have to say "I want it yesterday".'

Mrs C. J. Hales, of Egham, in Surrey, writes: 'A confusion similar to the one over "presently" exists in our household concerning "just now". My husband (born in Birmingham, educated at Solihull School and Manchester University) uses it to mean "very soon", "in a few minutes". I was born in Hampshire, educated at Chichester High School, Malvern Girls College and Oxford University, and I use it to mean "a short while ago". We are both in our mid-thirties.'

Mrs Aileen R. Evans, of Edgbaston, Birmingham, who was born in Scotland, writes of her experience with 'just now' on coming to England at the age of eighteen. When she heard it, she says, she found herself 'expecting immediate results that were not forthcoming. Not for the first time did I realise that in England "just now" meant precisely "*not* just now".

14 AUGUST 1983

P RESTIGIOUS, in the sense of having prestige, has come comparatively late to common usage (1950s), even later to full respectability. The OED entry prepared for publication in 1908 defines it as 'practising juggling or legerdemain; sleight of hand; cheating, deceptive, illusory'. Webster's Third New International (1961) has 'having an illustrious name or reputation; esteemed in general opinion'. The definition 'marked by illusion, conjuring or trickery', says Webster's, is 'archaic'. Prestige too began with a pretty bad reputation, not surprisingly in view of its derivation: the Latin *praestigiae*, juggler's tricks. The OED definitions and examples reflect the noun's progress: in the 1600s illusion and the like; more than a century later glamour, with its suggestion of magic power, comes in: in 1859 Charles Kingsley wrote of Elizabeth I's acceding to the throne 'with such a prestige as never sovereign came since the days when Isaiah sang his paean over young Hezekiah's accession'; the last definition is: 'Influence or reputation derived from previous character, achievements or associations'.

Now 'prestigious' too is gaining OED acceptance. Volume III (O to Scz) of the Supplement has yet to appear, but the Chief Editor of the Oxford English Dictionaries, Dr Robert Burchfield, kindly let me have the new definition: 'Having, showing or conferring prestige' − still cautious, but the examples are impressive: one goes back to 1913, in Joseph Conrad's *Chance* (also quoted by Webster's), '. . . the prestigious or the desirable things of the earth'.

And yet . . . Perhaps I am subscribing to what Professor Randolph Quirk calls the 'etymological fallacy', but I am still uneasy about the word (and about prestige too, for that matter). In the passage just quoted Conrad goes on to describe prestigious things as 'craved for by predatory natures'.

30 MARCH 1980

PRIVATISE.
Useful neologisms will survive, the others are not worth bothering about. But this one, I felt, was different. Besides the sheer ugliness of the word, what was wrong with 'denationalise'? After consulting the Treasury and other ministries I am not so sure. Denationalisation to me suggests outright disposal of government interest, as the Conservatives tried to do with steel in the 1950s and early 1960s. Privatisation, in contrast, covers part disposal as has happened with Cable and Wireless or British Aerospace.

So, although no one likes the word, no one has produced a better. Who fathered it? Some civil servants I spoke to suggested Mr Alfred Sherman, of the Centre for Policy Studies, the Conservative think-tank founded by Sir Keith Joseph and Mrs Thatcher in 1974. Mr Sherman neither claimed nor disclaimed paternity; he said he had been using the word since the mid-1970s.

It goes back further still. The first example in the files of the Oxford English Dictionaries (it will appear in the forthcoming Volume III, O to Scz, of A Supplement to the OED) is from the now defunct *News Chronicle* of 28 July 1959, which said that Dr Ludwig Erhard, chief architect of West Germany's post-war 'economic miracle', had 'selected the rich Preuffag mining concern for his first experiment in privatisation'.

13 DECEMBER 1981

Privy COUNCILLOR/COUNSELLOR. The inquiry into the origins of the Falklands crisis is being carried out by members of the Privy Council. But are they 'councillors' or 'counsellors'? Most newspapers, including *The Observer* and *The Times*, use '-cillor', as does the 1981 edition of the Oxford Dictionary for Writers and Editors. However, I have just acquired a copy of the dictionary 'reprinted with corrections, 1982', in which I find 'Privy Coun/cil, 'sellor'. Why the change, I asked the principal compiler, Dr Robert Allen. 'Because we wrote to the Privy Council', he replied. I then consulted the Clerk of the Council, Sir Neville Leigh, who was pleased at the change. In his opinion 'a Privy Counsellor is one who offers counsel as well as one who is a member of a council'. He added, 'But of course I could not claim that "councillor" was wrong.'

In its 'Privy Counsellor/Councillor' article, prepared for publication in 1908, the OED says 'from the 17th c. occasionally, and in the 19th c. often spelt "councillor" . . . but "counsellor" is the official as well as the historical form'.

(The Council is descended from the *Curia Regis* of Norman times and had its heyday under the Tudors. Membership today is mainly a mark of honour and goes to Cabinet Ministers and 'other distinguished persons'. Prince Philip became a member in 1951, Prince Charles in 1977. It meets in full only when a monarch comes to the throne or announces an intention to marry.)

1 AUGUST 1982

PRONUNCIATION. Everyman's English Pronouncing Dictionary (J. M. Dent) first appeared in 1917. Its compiler, Daniel Jones, Professor of Phonetics at London University, set out to record what was 'most usually heard in everyday speech' in southern English families 'whose menfolk had been educated at the great public boarding-schools'. He later abandoned public school pronunciation, PSP, in favour of received pronunciation, RP, roughly 'the educated pronunciation of London and the Home Counties'. (I have also heard it described as 'suburban Mayfair'.)

That information is from the fourteenth edition (1977). Professor A. C. Gimson, who now holds the chair and edits the dictionary (which, indeed, is known as 'Gimson' in the lexicographical trade), writes that although 'not all educated speakers use it nor can all who use it be safely described as "educated" ', he retains the term RP because it is a convenient name for an accent that remains generally acceptable.

I first heard of the dictionary when I wrote about the pronunciation of CONTROVERSY. Now I wonder how I ever did without it. Take Marseilles: *marsales* or *marsay*? (The second, 'athough wide used', is 'somewhat less common'.) Or Cirencester – the way you would expect or *cicester*? (The first is the one 'most usually heard in the town'.) In an uncertain world 'Gimson' is a great comfort.

2 AUGUST 1981

PURISTS and permissivists. Two useful contributions from Harpers Dictionary of Contemporary Usage (Harper and Row) to the never-ending (and a good thing too) debate on usage:

Lionel Trilling: I find righteous denunciation of the present state of the language no less dismaying than the present state of the language.

John Ciardi: Are there any enduring standards of English usage? I think there are only preferences, 'passionate preferences', as Robert Frost used to say . . . In the long run the usage of those who do not think about the language will prevail. Usages I resist will become acceptable. It is worth remembering that Swift inveighed against 'mob' as a vulgar corruption of *mobile vulgus*. He thought he was right to resist –

'mob' must have sounded to him as 'rep' for reputation does to me today. Yet English-speaking people decided he was wrong. It will not do to resist uncompromisingly. Yet those who care have a duty to resist. Changes that occur against such resistance are tested changes. The language is better for them — and for the resistance.

6 DECEMBER 1981

PUT-DOWNS (and how to pronounce them). 'Poetaster' ('a petty or paltry poet' — Oxford English Dictionary) is a word people are nervous about pronouncing: is the 'a' short or long? (It's short.) The Latin suffix -aster expresses resemblance, 'hence', the OED says, 'usually pejorative'. The force of this is seen in the French equivalent -âtre, literally '-ish', as in blanchâtre, whitish.

Admittedly 'poetaster' is not an everyday word, but the construction has any number of possibilities, to judge from the OED's other '-aster' words. One is 'criticaster' (also found in the Concise Oxford and American Webster's New Collegiate), which has the same connotations of paltriness and pettiness, and 'politicaster': 'The country is sick of the parliamentary squabbles of politicasters' (Pall Mall Gazette, 25 November 1892).

The phrase 'with respect' crops up as often as 'poetaster' does rarely — offhand I can't remember ever attending a conference when someone didn't use 'with respect' at least once — and has been so debased that it usually means (or sounds as if it means) just the reverse. Rather an offensive put-down, I always think. That hasn't happened (yet?) with pace, the ablative of pax, which still conveys a genuine feeling of deference: a polite, gentle put-down. But again people are uncertain of its pronunciation, some plumping for pahchay (as I did until taught otherwise) or pakhay. Dictionaries agree on paysee, although pahchay and pahkay are sometimes shown as alternatives.

12 JULY 1981

Putting on Dog.

Alan Watkins, *The Observer*'s Political Columnist, recently described the parliamentary Labour Party as, 'in one of the late Philip Toynbee's phrases, "putting on dog", asserting a supremacy or pre-eminence which it did not possess'. I too first met the phrase in a piece by Philip Toynbee, but that was not the sense in which I remembered his using it. He had described someone as *bien-pensant*, an expression I did not know and could not find in any dictionary; from the context it clearly did not mean 'well thinking'. It is indeed practically untranslatable (I have had a stab at explaining it — see entry), but this is not the place to go into it — some idea of its meaning can be had from a 1938 example in Volume I of A Supplement to the OED: '. . . all the French *bien-pensants* supported Franco'. The point here is that when I queried it with Philip he said with a sigh, 'I suppose I'm putting on dog.' According to Eric Partridge's A Dictionary of Slang and Unconventional English, 'to put on dog' means 'to put on "side", to show off'.

Paul Beale, who is revising Partridge, tells me that a character in novels of the late Gladys Mitchell is 'an omniscient, benevolent dragon of a lady detective, Dame Beatrice Lestrange Bradley. She has a young, bounding, upper-middle-class secretary/companion/assistant/stooge called Laura, a Scot. And Laura sometimes suggests that she should "put on the dog" — to dress smartly and "come the country lady" over some lower-class suspect, to use class as a frightener.' That, I suppose, is an assertion of superiority, if not supremacy, which goes some way to support Mr Watkins's use of the expression.

2 OCTOBER 1983

Mrs Jennifer Aebischer, of Forel, in Switzerland, asks: 'Could there be a connection between "putting on dog" and the French expression *avoir du chien*, meaning to have pluck, (of a lady) to be attractive, to have class?' I was about to reply thanking her for the expression, which I did not know, and saying that while it was a possible origin I did not think it a probable one. Then a letter arrived from Mr Alan Smith, co-author of *To Coin a Phrase* (Macmillan). He writes: 'When I was at school, in the Thirties and Forties, "dirty dog" and "rotten dog" were terms of real abuse. However, another tradition was evolving with "gay dog," "sly dog," or just "you dog" – "lucky dog" too – all implying the speaker's admiration for the "social" life he suspected the other person was leading.

'Flora Thompson in "Lark Rise" [1939] notes fond parents seeing their young boys setting off to work and "trying to walk like a man," saying, "Ain't he a young dog!" And only last month an article in *New Society* had ". . . but still the suspicion remains that the dullest politician is secretly a bit of a dog."

'All of which adds up to "dog" being a rough equivalent of "cutting a dash," "panache" even, in a small way. I feel that "putting on dog" is a natural growth from these usages (the "black dog on your shoulder" is, of course, another story).'

Mrs Aebischer's *avoir du chien*, if not in precisely the same class of expression, shares the note of approbation.

6 NOVEMBER 1983

London SW5

DEAR MR SILVERLIGHT, *I have heard 'dog' used by Americans, referring to a young woman not in the sense of 'bitch' but merely expressing disapproval – I forget whether it was her appearance or the fact that she commanded the company of two young men.*

Over to you

DORIS BAUM

St Michael's School, London, SE16

DEAR MR SILVERLIGHT, *My pupils here in Bermondsey tell me that 'dog' is always used pejoratively by them – it's about the lowest insult they use, especially to a girl, when it has connotations of 'loose morals'.*

Yours sincerely

(DR) TONY HARVEY,
Head of English Department

Leicester

DEAR SIR, *W. S. Gilbert used 'dog' implying admiration:* Trial by Jury *(1875) – 'The jury, shaking their forefingers at the judge, "Ah, sly dog!" (Bridesmaids repeat phrase towards jury.)'* Ruddigore *(1887) – Robin to Richard, 'You are, you know you are, you dog! a devil of a fellow — a regular out-and-out Lothario.'*

Yours faithfully

A. F. ORTON

*Q*UANTUM JUMP. 'Politicians will have to make a quantum jump in their thinking' — Mrs Shirley Williams. 'I began to wonder whether meeting up with the d'Amboises had been quite such a quantum jump after all' — Ted Peachum, the socially (and sexually) ambitious hero of Peter de Vries's *Consenting Adults*. It is all a long way from George Meredith's *The Ordeal of Richard Feverell*: 'Too much is decidedly bad', says the port-swilling solicitor, pouring himself a second glass in his office. 'But just the quantum makes men of us.'

The big change (quantum jump?) in the meaning of quantum took place in 1900 with Max Planck's Quantum Theory of physics. According to Planck, energy is emitted in radiation in discrete, or discontinuous amounts, which he called quanta. A quantum jump is the abrupt change in an atom from its 'ground state' to an 'excited state' and back again.

By transference it has also come to mean 'a sudden large increase or advance' (forthcoming Vol. III of A Supplement to the Oxford English Dictionary). Examples of this usage in the OED files date from the 1950s. Robert Junck, in his *Brighter than a Thousand Suns*, first published in Germany in 1956, quotes the American magazine *Fortune*: 'But the generals, if left to themselves, would never have been able to keep pace with this "quantum jump" in the technique of war.'

22 NOVEMBER 1981

*Q*UITE. 'I thought it was quite good.' 'I thought it was quite appalling.' Overhearing this exchange about a television programme aroused my interest in so flexible a word. 'The performance was quite excellent' (absolutely, to the greatest extent); 'The performance was *quite* good' (not bad); 'The performance was quite *good*' (better than expected); 'It was quite a performance' (remarkable); 'It was quite a long way' (considerable); 'It's not quite right' (something short of perfection: how short depends on how frank one is being — it could be just short, or very, very short); 'Quite!' (in a conversation); 'Exactly!' Quite a word, what with one thing and another.

22 FEBRUARY 1981

QUORATE.

The new City of London branch of the National Union of Journalists held its first meeting recently. Much time was spent debating the size of a quorum. Eventually the number 30 was accepted and we passed to other business. Suddenly a member — one of those who had passionately opposed 30 as being unrealistically high — declared that there were fewer than 30 of us still present and that the meeting was 'inquorate'.

I had not met the word before and none of my fellow union members could say with any certainty when the word was first used, so I telephoned the Oxford English Dictionaries. 'Quorate', I was told, would appear in the forthcoming Volume III of A Supplement to the OED. In their files was a reference to 'barely quorate' dated 1969, in *Pi*, the magazine of University College, London, Student Union. And in 1974 a letter to *The Times* described an Oxford students' meeting as an 'inquorate one', which 'therefore had no validity'. Useful words, both of them.

29 NOVEMBER 1981

RADDLED.

A review of a recent television play referred to 'a raddled old nun'; on 28 July the *Guardian* wrote of 'asbestos fibres in the raddled tissues of mesothelioma victims'; on 8 August *The Observer*, in an article on Margate, wrote of the 'raddled gentility of grander resorts'. I asked five colleagues what 'raddled' meant to them. They all reacted with some such word as 'worn' or 'ravaged'. One, however, led her list with 'painted' — which is what it originally meant: the OED definition of the verb is simply 'to paint . . . with raddle [red ochre]; to colour coarsely with rouge'.

Volume III of A Supplement to the OED, which came out in July, has this example: 'An "old Johnny" . . . like a funny raddled woman' (Galsworthy's *In Chancery*, 1922), but dictionaries were slow to note the development. The first I know to do so was Webster's Third International (1961), which gives as its third definition, 'pit, scar' − 'a crime-raddled neighborhood'. The 1964 Concise Oxford still had 'paint with raddle; plaster with rouge'; the 1965 Penguin had 'paint (face) with rouge'.

What interests me is an example in the original OED article that anticipates Galsworthy by more than two centuries: 'To revive the decay'd Red and White in their cheeks with raddle and chalk' (1699). This bears out my idea that words that undergo pejoration or amelioration have within them from the start the potential for such change. *(l wrt b chg: y OIH)*

Sheep farmers and country people generally are writing to me about 'raddled'. I knew from Hardy's *The Return of the Native* that farmers used raddle to mark sheep. Diggory Venn, the reddle-man ('reddle' is a variant, 'ruddle' another), 'whose vocation it was to supply farmers with redding', was always covered with the stuff. What I did not know was how farmers marked their sheep or, even more important, why. I know now.

Christine Richards, of Campbeltown, writes that she knows 'raddled' only in the 'down-to-earth context of tupping'. Rams, she explains, are raddled by painting their chests. The rams then raddle the ewes by serving them. Could this explain the pejoration 'raddles' has undergone? It could indeed. Eldon Smith, of Carmarthen, is in no doubt. 'Ewes which have been raddled', he writes, quoting a Gower shepherd as his source, and he adds, 'Loose women – well raddled!'

Varying the colour indicates when the raddling takes place. J. Alexander, of Dalbeattie, writes: 'Three colours are used, red for three weeks, blue for three weeks, then yellow. Obviously the "reds" will lamb first.'

12 SEPTEMBER 1982

REBUT/REFUTE/DENY.

I was always taught that 'rebut' and 'refute' were distinct in meaning. To rebut was to argue against: 'Mrs Thatcher firmly rebutted Mr Foot's claim that living standards had declined under the Conservatives.'

To refute was to disprove: 'Mrs Thatcher produced figures to refute Mr Foot's claim, etc.'

Dictionaries do not agree – even in the big Oxford, one of the definitions of 'rebut' is to disprove, with examples going back to 1817. I am not convinced. Despite lack of etymological support for my view, I cannot accept that the two words are synonymous.

However, what is agreed is that to use 'refute' for deny is incorrect – two dictionaries, Collins and the Oxford Paperback, have notes saying so specifically. But that usage seems to be increasing. Dr Robert Burchfield, Chief Editor of the Oxford Dictionaries, gloomily sees it possible that the distinction between 'refute' and 'deny' may become even more blurred in the next decade or two.

Usage is irresistible, and there is no profit in arguing with it. But I can't help regretting this particular example.

15 FEBRUARY 1981

REDUNDANT. 'No longer needed and therefore dismissed' (Chambers). But the word had another derogatory sense long before it was associated with jobs. I remember an English teacher who disliked redundant (i.e. unnecessary) words in writing more than 'dirty' words in conversation.

It has now acquired a benign meaning too. According to an unpublished paper on mapping the planets, 'the idea of sending two spacecraft on the Voyager probe is partly one of redundancy, i.e. if one fails the mission can still succeed'. (The other object is to vary the path of the probe slightly.) Dictionaries have the word in that sense, but I first saw it in practical use in Paul Ferris's civil defence article in *The Observer* of 12 July: 'The Army have "redundancies" built into their communications systems'; he too had not seen that use before.

Building such redundancies into a system – or a space probe, television set, calculator, what have you – ensures that it will go on functioning if a component fails; efficiency may be impaired, but total breakdown is avoided. This is 'graceful degradation' as opposed to 'catastrophic degradation'. It is a fine concept, and one that has emerged from new technology.

9 AUGUST 1981

York

DEAR MR SILVERLIGHT, 'Redundancy', in the sense of provision of back-up resources, originated in the context of communications engineering. The earliest occurrence that I know of is in a classic paper by Claude Shannon, published in 1948 in the Bell System Technical Journal. This paper was of profound theoretical importance — comparable with Einstein on relativity — and transformed communications engineering overnight. In case you should think that all this is rather esoteric, I can tell you that the effects of the paper spread rapidly through the scientific and engineering community in the early 1950s, and certainly by 1960 had become common currency in telecommunications courses in universities and technical colleges.

I do not know when the word was first used in this sense in the general press, but I should imagine it was during the 1960s. But this was undoubtedly preceded by use in New Scientist, Wireless World and other popular scientific periodicals.

Yours sincerely

BILL FREEMAN

Department of Linguistics, University of Cambridge

DEAR MR SILVERLIGHT, Your breathless report on the newly-minted meaning of 'redundant' ('unpublished paper' implies that you are mediating between the technocrats and the ignorant masses) commits the age-old folk-linguistic howler — viz. 'if I only heard it in this sense on July 12, then it must be new'. Perfectly understandable reflex, but someone writing a column on words really should do a little more homework — at any rate than asking the man working on the adjoining page.

Taking a book on communication of the shelf at random, I read, 'Every language, if it is to be reliable, must be redundant' (in precisely the required sense). This book, G. Miller's Language and Communication, was printed in 1951, and in ms form around in 1946.

It is certainly a fine concept, but not one that has emerged — as you half-bakedly surmise — from NASA or Silicon Valley. It goes back at least to the early work of Weaver and Shannon; to make other than a rough guess would need more than a chat with Paul Ferris.

Yours,

I. A. BOAL

R̲EFERENCES. You will find it a very good practice always to verify your references, sir!' — Dr Martin Joseph Routh (1755–1854). Sometimes it's not so easy. An Aims of Industry advertisement in the *Spectator* of 3 July contained this quotation: 'The only thing necessary for the triumph of evil is for good men to do nothing' (Burke). The American columnist William Safire tells in his book *On Language* of his experiences after using the quotation in an article in the *New York Times*. A reader asked him for the source. He looked in Bartlett's Familiar Quotations, fourteenth edition, and 'there it was, page 454, cited in a letter . . . to William Smith on January 9, 1795. Condescendingly I dropped Mr Long a note telling him to do his homework.' 'It's not in that letter', Mr Long replied. A long, unsuccessful search followed. Mr Safire comments sadly, 'The only thing necessary for the triumph of misquotation is for wise guys to do nothing.'

I consulted Conor Cruise O'Brien, who edited the Pelican Classics edition of Burke's *Reflections on the Revolution in France*. 'He *could* have said it', Dr O'Brien replied, 'but I have read the published works twice and cannot find it. The assumption must be that he didn't.'

In the fifteenth edition of Bartlett's the source of the quotation has been replaced by a footnote saying merely 'Attributed'.

22 AUGUST 1982

R̲EMIT as a noun, meaning terms of reference, and pronounced *rē-mit*, is an unfamiliar, unloved word outside bureaucratic circles, but it is a useful one: one word in place of three. Examples in the files of the forthcoming Volume III of A Supplement to the Oxford English Dictionary, O to Scz, date from 1963. Here is one: 'The architect cannot have understood the terms of the re-mit . . . given by the all-party committee on accommodation' (*New Statesman*). The noun is not in the old Concise Oxford (1964) or in the Shorter Oxford (1933). Interestingly, it does appear in the much older OED — one definition (entry prepared for publication in 1906), with an example dated 1719, is not unlike present usage, but pronunciation has changed.

The OED has *rimi·t*, like the verb, thus bracketing it with those words that emphasise the second syllable both when used as a noun and a verb (others are 'design' and 'divide'). A larger group of such words (e.g. 'contrast', 'ferment', 'permit') change the emphasis according to the use, emphasising the second syllable as a verb and the first as a noun. So, nowadays, does 'remit' — as the *New Statesman* indicated in the example quoted.

22 MARCH 1981

RULE THE ROAST/ROOST.

How did 'roost' replace 'roast', asks a reader, Eric Whitton, of Gipsy Hill, in south-east London. 'The OED does not even recognise the existence of the latter.' Fowler, in the first edition of Modern English Usage (1926), writes: 'Most unliterary persons say "roost" and not "roast"; I have just inquired of three such, and been informed that they have never heard of "rule the roast," and that the reference is to a cock keeping his hens in order.' Against this, in seven of the eight pre-eighteenth-century examples quoted in the OED, the spelling is 'rost' or 'roste'. 'The OED philologists', Fowler goes on, 'would tell us that "rost(e)" could represent Old-French *rost* (roast) and could not represent Old-English *hrost* (roost).' (The second edition of Modern English Usage (1965), revised by Sir Ernest Gowers, comments that 'roost' is commoner and more intelligible.)

Vol. III of A Supplement to the OED has this example, dated 1794: 'They say she rules the Roost, it is a pity, I like her Husband vastly' (from the quarterly magazine of William and Mary College, in Virginia). Another example with 'roost', dated 1893, is from the *Boston Journal*, all of which suggests that the change could have begun in the United States. Among modern desk dictionaries the New Collins Concise has 'rule the roost (or roast)'; the Concise Oxford has 'rule the roast or roost'; Chambers has 'rule the roast (mistakenly roost)'. Until receiving Mr Whitton's letter, if a latter-day Fowler had asked me about 'rule the roast', I would have been among the unliterary lot.

30 JANUARY 1983

SMEAR

SMEAR. A difficult word to avoid in newspapers these days: 'Mgr Bruce Kent . . . attacked Mr Winston Churchill . . . for his involvement with people trying to "smear" CND' — *The Times*, 29 April; 'Mr Churchill said, "[Mgr Kent] is seeking to smear me and my colleagues in the Conservative Party by alleging a smear campaign" ' — *The Times*, 30 April; 'Morell [Hitler's doctor] narrowly escaped execution by the SS when rivals smeared him' — *Daily Mail*, 5 May; '. . . in Egypt Heykal . . . has been denounced for allegedly smearing the late President Sadat' — *The Observer*, 8 May.

'Smear' goes back to Anglo-Saxon, Old High German, etc., in which it meant fat or grease, its obsolete sense in English; the modern Scandinavian word means butter. The pejorative sense of the verb ('. . . implying something base or discreditable' — OED) goes back at least to the mid-1500s: an 1879 example reads, 'She would not try to smear his memory with any falsehoods now.'

I assumed that the modern, political sense dated from the days of McCarthyism, and the guess was supported by an example in Webster's Third New International (1961): 'people . . . whom he has smeared by all sorts of distortions and misrepresentations' — Elmer Davis, a noted opponent of Joe McCarthy. In fact that usage is older. The forthcoming Volume IV of A Supplement to the Oxford English Dictionary has this example, dated 1936: '. . . the Republicans began calling this line of attack the "smear Hoover" campaign'.

The Supplement has another, chilling usage I did not know: 'To thrash or kill; wipe out by bombing: "We can smear every base, every industrial complex, once and for all" ' (P. Frank, *Seven Days to Never*, 1957).

15 MAY 1983

SHAMBLES

SHAMBLES. In 1972, on the Saturday after the massacre of Israeli athletes at the Munich Olympic Games, we were struggling for a headline on *The Observer*'s background story.

It was edition time, and the Printer was getting edgy. Suddenly someone suggested, 'What about "The Shambles of Fuerstenfeldbruck"?' (the suburb where the killings had taken place). Why shambles? On the News Desk was a Shorter Oxford English Dictionary, where we found, 'place of carnage or wholesale slaughter; a scene of blood.' What I have just realised is how recently the word acquired its present general sense of 'utter confusion'.

The OED's first definition of the singular 'shamble' (entry prepared in 1913) is 'stool, footstool', from the Latin *scamellum*, a diminutive of *scamnum*. bench. Then 'table . . . for exposing goods for sale'; 'table . . . for the sale of meat'; 'place where meat (or occas. fish) is sold, a flesh- or meat-market.' Next, in the plural, comes '. . . slaughter-house'; finally, 'place of carnage etc.' as in the Shorter.

In 1934, the year after the OED was completed and the Shorter came out, the Concise Oxford had 'butcher's slaughter-house, scene of carnage'. By 1944 the Concise's addenda had, 'Shambles (also, loosely, esp. in journalistic use) mess, muddle, with no implication of blood or death'; the 1964 Concise added that to the main entry. In 1976 the addition became merely, 'colloq. mess, muddle' — no crack at journalists, it will be noted.

The forthcoming Vol. IV of A Supplement to the OED has: 'In more general use, a scene of disorder or devastation . . . orig. US.' An example from Evelyn Waugh's *Put Out More Flags* (1942) reads: 'Alastair learned, too, that all schemes ended in a "shambles" which did not mean, as he had feared, a slaughter, but a brief restoration of individual freedom of movement.' (The Supplement's following entry is 'shambolic': 'chaotic, disorderly . . . ' with the observation, 'reported to be "in common use" in 1958 — Ed.')

18 SEPTEMBER 1983

Blackrock, Dublin

The first performance of Mr Handel's Messiah *was held in the Antient Concert Rooms in Fishamble Street, Dublin, in 1742.*

Fishamble St. is in the old city area, near Christ Church Cathedral.

NORAH DRAPER

Mrs E. Henry, of Ruislip, in Middlesex, writes to ask if The Shambles in York has a link with some event involving 'carnage or wholesale slaughter' as in the OED definition of the word.

Yes, but not of human beings. An early sense of 'shambles'

is 'table or stall for the sale of meat'; areas where butchers gathered came to be known as 'shambles', and many towns all over the country had streets of that name. The earliest OED example in that sense, dated 1440, in the entry 'flesh-shambles', reads: 'All the folks of the salsemakers [sauce-makers?] . . . without [i.e. outside] the Flesschameles' − from the York Mysteries, the plays performed by the crafts, or mysteries, of York on Corpus Christi (Thursday after Trinity Sunday).

Since every butcher did his own slaughtering next to where he traded, it is easy to see how 'shambles' took on its present sense of mess or muddle. Mr James Dunning, who is writing a book on the origins of the family butcher, says the Worshipful Company of Butchers has records between 1331 and 1423 of the butchers of St Nicholas Shambles, in the City of London, being fined for not disposing of the entrails etc. 'to proper places'. Miss A. M. Kennet, the Chester Archivist, quotes an 1833 reference to the old Shambles as being 'highly discreditable to the city'. Pip, in *Great Expectations*, describes Smithfield as 'that shameful place . . . all asmear with filth and fat'.

There are other distasteful associations. 'Flesh-shambles' also meant brothel: 'Venice . . . is counted to be the best flesh-shambles of Italy' (1608). Mrs Margaret Glaser, of north-west London, quotes Desdemona: 'I hope my noble lord esteems me honest.' Othello: 'O, ay; as summer flies are in the shambles, /That quicken even with blowing' (where 'blowing' meant the blowfly's depositing of its eggs in raw flesh).

9 OCTOBER 1983

S POKEN WORD (The), a BBC publication by Dr Robert Burchfield, Chief Editor of the Oxford English Dictionaries, has more good sense and useful information in its 40 pages than many books on English usage four and five times as long.

Ever since its foundation the BBC has been much concerned with pronunciation − rightly, in view of the influence of broadcasting on the way we speak. Paul Ferris, in his radio programme 'English as She is Broadcast', quoted the Poet Laureate Robert Bridges on 'miniature' in 1926: 'I have no opinion except to *forbid* "minnycher".' This guide for broadcasters is the result of the Corporation's latest bout of agonising.

I like the footnotes. On 'hopefully' in the sense of 'it is hoped': 'Used only by the brave or by young people unaware of public hostility to the use. Fanatically opposed by purists.' Or this, on the recommendations to stress the second syllable of 'sonorous': 'This traditional pronunciation is now fairly rapidly being replaced by one with the first syllable stressed . . .' Most of all I like Dr Burchfield's refusal to be doctrinaire: 'English grammar is a complicated system never quite mastered even by the best speakers of English. The best writers and speakers avoid grammatical solecisms by keeping clear of areas which contain problems that would reveal their own uncertainties.' The guide is a perfect Christmas stocking present.

8 NOVEMBER 1981

SRI LANKA. A feature in *The Observer* recently noted the renaming of Ceylon in 1972 to Sri Lanka, 'which means Resplendent Island'. Mr S. C. Crowther-Smith, of Oxford, suggests that the country's inhabitants 'have always called their country Sri Lanka' – 'Ceylon', he points out, sounds like the first two syllables of 'Sri Lanka'.

I put the idea to Mr Christopher Reynolds, lecturer in Sinhalese at the School of Oriental and African Studies, at the same time asking him about Resplendent Island. Lanka, he replied has always been the Sinhalese name. The names used in other languages – Si-lan (Chinese), Ceilão (Portuguese), Zeilan (Dutch), Ceylon (English) – all come from 'Sinhala', which is what the majority community, the Sinhalese, call themselves. He is less certain about Resplendent Island. *Sri* is an honorific (in India it is used like 'Mr') and so could mean resplendent. Lanka does not mean island: it is a proper noun and means Lanka. However, the sense of island *is* found in the name by which the Arabs knew it, Sarandib: *dib*, says Mr Reynolds, means island. That word rang a bell.

'Serendipity', the facility of making happy and unexpected discoveries by accident, comes from Serendip, 'a former name of Ceylon' (OED). In 1754 Horace Walpole wrote that he had formed the word 'upon the title of the fairy-tale "The Three Princes of Serendip," the heroes of which were always making

95

discoveries, by accidents and sagacity, of things they were not in quest of'.

3 JULY 1983

START.

President Reagan last weekend launched his proposal for negotiations with the Soviet Union on the reduction of nuclear weapons. It goes under the name of START: Strategic Arms Reduction Talks. (The acronym was coined by Mr Eugene Rostow, one of the late President Johnson's more hawkish advisers during the Vietnam War, now director of the US Arms Control and Disarmament Agency.) It replaces SALT – Strategic Arms Limitation Talks – which produced the SALT Treaties. SALT I limited anti-ballistic missiles. SALT II was intended to limit strategic weapons, but was not ratified by the US Senate because of Afghanistan.

START was to have got under way last winter. In November President Reagan announced: 'To symbolise this fundamental change in direction we will call these negotiations START.' Then came the suppression of Poland's Solidarity movement and the imposition of military rule. The Americans, holding the Russians responsible, put the proposal on one side.

The significance of the new approach, according to the Reagan men, is the positive *reduction* of START in contrast with the mere *limitation* of SALT. Some people in Washington and elsewhere take the distinction with more than a pinch of salt. My question is: Could START finish with END, European Nuclear Disarmament, as advocated by Mr E. P. Thompson and others?

16 MAY 1982

STATURE.

Mr Paul Pearce, of Doncaster, writes apropos my reference to Trollope's 'stature' (see NAVVY): 'I have noticed an increasing use of the word, which I have always taken to mean the size or height of a man or animal, to mean status or standing . . . Is this usage correct, and if it is correct, is it desirable when we already have two more than adequate words to say the same thing?'

Modern desk dictionaries give 'stature' as position gained by development or achievement as well as in the sense of bodily height; the first OED example of the figurative usage is dated 1834. But what interests me is the use of the word in the Bible: 'Till we all come . . . unto the measure of the stature of the fulness of Christ' (Ephesians iv 13). The word in the original Greek is *helikia*, of which the first meaning in Liddell and Scott is 'time of life, age', then 'prime of life, manhood, maturity' (of women 'womanhood'); the fourth meaning given is 'of the body, *stature* as being a sign of age'.

All this seems to have worried translators. My Authorised Version has a note giving 'age' as an alternative to 'stature' in the Ephesians passage, which in the New English Bible reads: '. . . to mature manhood, measured by nothing less than the full stature of Christ'.

I do not agree with Mr Pearce about 'status' and 'standing'. 'Status', besides being somewhat tarnished by the expression 'status symbol,' has a legal connotation and 'standing' a social connotation. But I am grateful to him for putting me on to an ambiguity that goes back to St Paul and, indeed, to Homer, eight centuries earlier.

16 JANUARY 1983

S͟Y͟N͟T͟O͟N͟Y͟. A resonant word. So resonant that it was something of an anti-climax to see it defined in the OED as: '*Electr.* The condition of being syntonic', i.e. 'denoting a system of wireless telegraphy in which the transmitting and receiving instruments are accurately "tuned" so that the latter responds only to the frequency emitted by the former.' That was very different from the context in which I had first met the word: '. . . the optimum mixture, balance or syntony of the major forces and processes of the body' — from *Celestial Lancets* by Lu Gwei-Djen and Joseph Needham. (See *KRASIS*.)

I consulted Dr Needham. In using 'syntony' in that sense, he said, he was thinking of 'muscle tone', muscles in tonic condition, the opposite of flaccidity. Etymologically this was most interesting. The Greek lexicon's first definition of *tonos*, from which 'tone' is derived, is 'that which tightens a thing'. Adding *syn-*, with, you get *syntonos*, stretched tight; of persons, eager, vehement — all of which reflects another meaning of *tonos*: force, exertion of force, intensity. There is still another meaning of *syntonos*, in harmony, which hardly seems to fit with all that tension. But it does fit. Something that is stretched, a length of animal gut, say, will give off a sound, or tone, which is still another meaning of *tonos*. Different tensions will produce different tones which, if correctly 'tuned', will be in harmony.

Modern Greek usage in this context is interesting too. The second most powerful person in a Greek Government is the Minister of National Economy: until recently the department was known as the Ministry of Coordination, or *Syntonismós*. A last touch: the sign on that word *Syntonismós*, indicating the stressed syllable, is called the *tonos*.

18 DECEMBER 1983

TASK FORCE.

A reader asks: 'When was this expression new, 1982?' It is older than that but I doubt if it has ever had as much exposure, at least in this country, as it has had this year. It can rarely have been out of the headlines from 3 April, the day after the Argentines invaded the Falklands, until the Argentine surrender at Port Stanley on 14 June.

It originated in the United States in the Second World War: the first example in the files of the Oxford English Dictionaries is, 'A division of Marines and one of infantry as a potential AEF "task force" for action overseas' – *Time*, 23 June 1941. By 1944 it was in the addenda of the Concise Oxford: 'Specially organised unit for a special task.' That definition is interesting. As the *Time* example indicates, a task force was very much a military affair. Yet with the war still in progress, here is a lexicographer realising the expression's potential and anticipating its extended non-military sense. The first example of this later use in the Oxford files is: 'The work stoppage resulted from an attempt by the city to try out a "task force" system of collections' – *Richmond* (Va.) *Times–Dispatch*, 1 March 1949. Webster's Seventh New Collegiate (1965) still emphasises the military association: 'A temporary grouping esp. of armed forces units under one leader for the purpose of accomplishing a definite objective.' In the Eighth New Collegiate (1975) the words 'esp. of armed forces' are dropped.

Now I seem to be meeting it more and more often. Two examples: 'One of President Reagan's first actions was to appoint a task force on violent crime' – *The Observer*, 25 July; 'Labour should appoint a task force against low pay' – *The Times*, 5 August.

15 AUGUST 1982

TENNIS.

In 1888 the *St James's Gazette* wrote: 'It is melancholy to see a word which has held its own for centuries gradually losing its connotation. Such a word is "tennis", by which nine out of ten persons today would understand the game of recent invention played on an unconfined court' (OED).

The 'game of recent invention' was *lawn* tennis, introduced some 14 years earlier and called 'Sphairistike', from the Greek for 'playing at ball'; A. J. Balfour, himself a noted player in his time, is credited with coining its present name. The centuries-old game mentioned in the *St James's Gazette* was *royal* tennis, played in a walled court. This game, introduced into Florence by French knights in 1325, was known to the Italians as *tenes*; the OED's first example in English, spelt 'tenetz', is dated 1399.

Three words that have always puzzled me until writing this article are 'deuce', 'love' and 'let'. 'Deuce' is from *à deux*, in Italian *a due*, 'denoting that the two sides have each gained three points (called "forty"), in which case *two* successive points must be gained to win the game' (OED). 'Love' comes from *l'oeuf*, since an egg looks like a zero. 'Let' is from the old sense of the word as in 'let or hindrance', or, 'I'll make a ghost of him that lets me' (*Hamlet*).

20 JUNE 1982

TONGUE IN CHEEK.

A reader has asked about this expression. What it means is well enough known: to speak ironically or insincerely. But no one seems to know where it comes from. It is certainly very old which, perhaps, explains why its origin is so obscure. The forthcoming fourth and final volume of A Supplement to the Oxford English Dictionary will have in it this quotation from Tobias Smollett's *Roderick Random* (1748): 'I signified my contempt for her by thrusting my tongue in my cheek.' Not very relevant for my purposes, but interesting.

Dr Desmond Morris, author of *The Naked Ape* and other works on animal behaviour, offers this suggestion: 'Someone, sometime, after saying something he (or she) didn't really mean, must have put his (or her) tongue in his (or her) cheek as though saying, "I must stop my tongue from saying that," or, "I shouldn't have said that" – a gesture, indeed, rather like clapping one's hand over one's mouth.'

7 NOVEMBER 1982

TROTSKYIST/TROTSKYITE – which to use? It can depend on your politics. The Oxford English Dictionary, after listing a selection of words including Wycliffite, Brontëite, Darwinite, Luddite and Parnellite, says, 'These have a tendency to be depreciatory, being mostly given by opponents and seldom acknowledged by those to whom they are applied.' If I hear someone described as a Trotskyite, I assume disapproval on the part of the user. People who believe in Trotskyism (especially Trotsky's concept of worldwide revolution as opposed to Stalin's belief in socialism in one country) call themselves Trotskyists. (*Private Eye*, with its insistence on 'homosexualist' for 'homosexual', manages to make '-ist' derogatory too.)

Questions continue to nag at me. Why is the adherent of Marxism a Marxist, or Calvinism a Calvinist, and never a Marxite or Calvinite, but the adherent of Luddism always a Luddite and never a Luddist? Again, what determines whether the practitioner of a skill is an '-ist' (agriculturalist, pianist, cyclist, journalist, bigamist) or an '-er' – astronomer, biographer, executioner?

As Dr Johnson said, 'It may be reasonably imagined, that what is so much in the power of men as language, will very often be capriciously conducted.'

30 AUGUST 1981

TWITCHERS and TWERLIES. On 6 June newspapers carried reports of twitchers ('bird-watchers who travel hundreds of miles to record sightings of rare birds') from all over the country invading a farmer's land in Norfolk.

100

On 9 June a letter appeared in *The Times* from a bird-watcher who had never sighted the 'rare and neologistic species' Twitcher. On 11 June came the reply that it 'is fully documented in Bill Oddie's "Little Black Bird Book" ' (Methuen 1980): '. . . he literally twitches with the excitement of it all.'

A neologism is often disapproved of, says Webster's Eighth New Collegiate Dictionary, 'because of its newness or barbarousness'. What about my other word, which is so new that I am not even certain how to spell it. A friend has just qualified for a GLC Elderly Person's travel permit, which allows free bus trips between 9.30 and 4.30 and after 7. 'Oh', said a bus conductress he knows, 'so you've joined the "twerlies".' 'Twerlies?' 'They're always asking, "Am I too early?" '

I'm all for neologising. If the word is really useful it will survive. If not, it won't.

21 JUNE 1981

UP TO/DOWN TO. Mrs Frances Wilkinson, of Meston, near Ilkley, writes: 'When did "up to" become "down to"? I used to tell my sons it was up to Daddy whether we went for a picnic. They tell *their* children it is down to Mummy. Brian Widlake (Radio 4) says it is "up to the Government". Sue Lawley (Nationwide) says it is "down to the doctors".'

I don't know − when did the expression come in?

7 NOVEMBER 1982

Letters in response to words are as capricious as they are gratifying: I never know when a word is going to strike a chord. 'Down to' certainly struck one: letters have poured in. Sources suggested include the worlds of crime, jazz and used-car dealing. Mr Marshall Colman gives this neat example: 'You can put this broken window *down to* the cricketers and it is *up to* them to repair it.' I like this one, from Mr Ian Mikardo, MP: 'I can't tell you (or Mrs Wilkinson) when "down to" came in, but I can tell you where it came from, which is on-course betting. If you go up to a bookmaker in the ring to have a fiver on Red Rum, he will take your money, give you a ticket and say to his clerk, "Red Rum twenty pounds to five, ticket number eighty-eight." But if you are a regular customer, to whom he gives credit, his instructions will be, "Red Rum, twenty pounds to five, down to Silverlight." The import of "down to" is, "booked down to the responsibility of Silverlight".'

5 DECEMBER 1982

Horsell, Surrey

DEAR MR SILVERLIGHT, *There would seem to be a clear difference of meaning between the uses of 'down to' and 'up to'. If purchasing something in a store where I had an account, I would ask, 'Please put it down to me', meaning that the purchase price of the article should be written down as a debit against my name. The amount is put* down *to me, but when I pay is* up *to me.*

GILL BENNETT

V ALENTINE.

What could be easier, I thought, than writing about Valentine's Day? I was wrong. For one thing, the OED says Valentine was the name of *two* early Italian saints commemorated on 14 February. One was a priest and physician, the other a bishop. But just to be difficult, the Oxford Dictionary of the Christian Church says it is 'possible' that the two legends refer to one person after all.

What has all this to do with choosing sweethearts and sending cards (the valentine, Britannica says, was 'probably the first of all greeting cards')? Nothing. The traditions seem to be connected with Februs, the great Roman feast of purification and expiation (also Lupercalia), held on 15 February. Goats and dogs were sacrificed and their skins cut into *februa*, or purifiers, with which priests ran about lashing at people. Women believed that a cut with a lash 'removed barrenness' (Everyman's Encyclopaedia).

Then there is the medieval belief that birds start mating in mid-February – Chaucer's 'For this was on seynt Volentynys day Whan euery bryd comyth there to chese his make' ('Parlement of Foules', the long poem that begins, 'The lyf so short, the crafte so long to lerne').

One of Shakespeare's two gentlemen of Verona is named Valentine. And Ophelia, in her madness, sings: 'Tomorrow is Saint Valentine's Day/All in the morning betime/And I a maid

at your window/To be your Valentine'; the ribaldry that follows
only heightens the pathos.

how very true

13 FEBRUARY 1983

VIABLE. People, including writers I respect, have taken
against this word. I cannot think why. It comes from the Latin
vita, life, through the French *vie*, and was first used in the
nineteenth century, by doctors who spoke of a viable foetus, or
a viable new-born child, one capable of life; then by naturalists,
who spoke of viable seed – capable of germinating.

Then, by a perfectly natural extension, it was applied to
inanimates, such as a company or a regime – if it is logical to
speak of a firm that is dying, why not one that is viable
commercially? Or a regime that is viable politically? How else
could you say it so succinctly.

The most imaginative use of the word I have seen is
Anthony Burgess's in the book pages of *The Observer* last
month. The heroine of *La Dame aux Camélias*, he wrote, 'wore
white camellias on the viable days of the month, red roses on
the others'.

6 JANUARY 1980

Annecy, France

DEAR SIR, *My students would like to know: viable foetuses = which
can live; viable new-born = who can live; viable seed = which will live
(not die); viable regime = which will live (not die); viable days =
which will live . . . in her memory? Is this what A. Burgess means?*

RORY O'SULLIVAN

DEAR MR O'SULLIVAN, *I suspect that Mr Burgess had in mind
something more practical than days that would live in the memory of
La Dame aux Camélias. On her non-viable days it would not have
been feasible (another sense of 'viable' often met nowadays) for her to
follow her calling.*

Yours sincerely

JOHN SILVERLIGHT

W̲A̲P̲S̲ is what an Anglo-Saxon would have called a 'wasp'. Before Chaucer 'birds' were 'brids'. Queen Elizabeth I wrote 'shirlest' for 'shrillest'. The changes, says Mr John Ayto, of Brighton, were the result of metathesis, the swapping over of two sounds within a word. He writes, apropos the roughly contemporary process misdivision (e.g. 'newt' for 'an ewt', see EYAS): 'While most examples ("waps" etc) are buried under successive layers of linguistic sediment, there are survivors: Scots make "girdle" cakes on what the English call "griddles"; "southron" is poetic diction for "southern"; "ax" is Mummerset for "ask"; many Scots say "modren" for "modern"; metathesis explains why the German equivalents of "horse" and "burn" are *ross* and *brennen* (a German word for "brandy" is *Weinbrand*, burnt wine).

'It usually happened like this: "through" in Old English was (to spell it the modern way) *thorgh*; an extra vowel got inserted after the "r" – from which we get "thorough." Then it came to be stressed on the second syllable, and eventually the first vowel disappeared, hence "through." Perhaps in time the Irish, Scots and north-east English "fillum" will turn into "flim." '

There is also aphesis, the loss of a short, unaccented vowel at the beginning of a word – 'squire' ('esquire') or 'down' ('adown'). The word 'aphesis' was coined, in 1880, by the great James Murray himself, chief compiler of the Oxford English Dictionary. I like 'peach', from 'appeach', to accuse (now 'impeach') but also to inform against. Remember Peachum, the receiver in 'The Beggar's Opera', who added to his income by informing against his clients?

13 NOVEMBER 1983

Weston-super-Mare

What does Mr Ayto mean by 'Mummerset'? 'Ax' is Somerset for 'ask', so is 'wops' or 'wopsy' for 'wasp'.
London West Indian kids say 'flim' already.

J̲O̲A̲N̲ H̲A̲R̲R̲I̲S̲S̲O̲N̲

DEAR SIR, The change from 'fillum' to 'flim' has already firmly established itself in Antigua, in the West Indies. Employed some four years ago on a Universal Production 'The Island', starring Michael Caine, the local population almost invariably referred to our work as 'the Flim'.

Sincerely,
D. G. SUTTON

PS. In my Channel Island youth, on our way to the pictures we would almost invariably buy a packet of what in those days we called 'crips', though we only had salted, there being no onion or bacon flavours at that time.

WEBSTER'S Collegiate has for years been my favourite desk dictionary, partly because it keeps me in touch with American usage. It also contains more information than our 'concise' dictionaries: biographical and geographical names are given; there are illustrations. The Collins English (1979), was modelled on this type of 'campus' dictionary.

The ninth edition of the Collegiate, which came out in this country last week, distributed by Longman, has two new features. One is the dating of the entry of words into the language. Not as full as the OED's, naturally: it won't tell you when, say, 'shambles' took on its present sense of mess or muddle (1920s), but it's fun to learn that the despised 'hospitalise' goes back to 1899. (I disagree with the dating of 'acid rain', 1976. As readers will know (see ACID RAIN), it goes back to 1872.)

The other innovation is notes on disputed usages. Some of these notes may well themselves be disputed − which would be nothing new for Webster's. The two-volume Third International caused a nationwide scandal when it came out, in 1961, with such words as 'ain't', 'piss-poor' and 'irregardless'. A bishop wrote: 'The greatest of all American dictionaries been corrupted at center.'

The ninth edition of the Collegiate is more permissive than ever. Take 'enormity', which 'need not carry overtones of moral transgression'. De Quincey is quoted: '. . . the enormity of his learned acquisitions'. Or 'flaunt' as meaning 'flout',

105

which, it is suggested, may not be all that heinous a semantic sin, although there is a warning that 'many people' would consider such usage 'a mistake'. Eyebrows are going to be raised.

23 OCTOBER 1983

YOMPING. The 1914–18 War produced 'strafe'. We got 'blitz' from the Second World War. In Vietnam the Americans 'zapped' the Cong. Earlier this month several newspapers carried a pooled dispatch from the *Daily Telegraph*'s man in the Falklands reporting that British troops were 'yomping' towards Port Stanley – 'marching, humping anything up to 120 lb of equipment and all the arms needed for attack at the end of the trek'.

The source of 'yomping' is obscure. Lexicographers have not heard of it. A Royal Marine officer at Portsmouth said it was in use when he joined the corps ten or twelve years ago. The editor of the corps journal *Globe and Laurel* said it began turning up in articles five years ago.

For some years Marine Commandos have been training in the far north of Norway. Laplanders live there and a Norwegian diplomat told us that one of their tribal heroes is Yompa, famous for his prowess at hunting and 'fighting the forces of evil'. It would be nice to think that the Commandos got the word from Yompa but I doubt it. My theory, not put forward too seriously, is that in Scandinavian languages 'j' is pronounced like 'y' so that 'Jump to it' pronounced facetiously would sound like 'Yump (or Yomp) to it.' Whence 'yomping'.

13 JUNE 1982

Rayleigh, Essex

DEAR MR SILVERLIGHT, I think you are correct in attributing 'yomping' to the Scandinavian difficulty in pronouncing 'j'. In the world of rallying the Finns and Swedes are supreme – well, almost – and the word 'yump' for 'jump' has passed into rallying literature. It is often used in detailed route instructions at a particular map reference, e.g. 'bad muddy yump at 634829'. So 'yumping' to indicate hazardous travel over difficult terrain is entirely logical.

Yours etc.

M. R. BLACKMORE

Ashington, Sussex

DEAR SIR, *Your theory on 'yomping', while 'not put forward too seriously', is not very far from the truth. In* The Motorist's Bedside Book (*ed. Anthony Harding, Batsford, 1972*) *you will find on page 55, under the photograph of a Saab with all four wheels in the air, the caption 'Yumping — Swedish rally, 1969'.*

Yours faithfully,

DAVID L. SIMPKIN

---

13 King's Bench Walk, Temple, EC4

DEAR SIR, *The Swedish word* jumpa, *pronounced not unlike* yumpa, *means to jump from icefloe to icefloe.*

Yours faithfully,
JONATHAN FERRIS